More Easter cracked

© Scripture Union 2012
First published 2012
ISBN 978 1 84427 714 8

Scripture Union
207–209 Queensway, Bletchley, Milton Keynes, MK2 2EB
Email: info@scriptureunion.org.uk
Website: www.scriptureunion.org.uk

Performing Licence
If you wish to perform any of the sketches in this book, you are free to do so without charge, providing the performance is undertaken in an amateur context. The purchase of this book constitutes a licence granting the right to perform the pieces for no financial gain. Those wishing to engage in commercial or professional performances should make a separate approach in writing to Scripture Union.

Scripture quotations are from the Contemporary English Version published by HarperCollins*Publishers* © 1991, 1992, 1995 American Bible Society.

British Library Cataloguing-in-Publication Data
A catalogue record of this book is available from the British Library.

Printed and bound in Singapore by Tien Wah Press.

Cover design: Paul Airy
Compiler: Christine Wright
Artists: Andy Robb, Tim Charnick, Gill Chelski, Eira Reeves, Neil Pinchbeck, Sue Cony, Mike Kazybrid Pauline Adams, Sonia Canals

Scripture Union is an international Christian charity working with churches in more than 130 countries.

Thank you for purchasing this book. Any profits from this book support SU in England and Wales to bring the good news of Jesus Christ to children, young people and families and to enable them to meet God through the Bible and prayer.

Find out more about our work and how you can get involved at:

www.scriptureunion.org.uk (England and Wales)
www.suscotland.org.uk (Scotland)
www.suni.co.uk (Northern Ireland)
www.scriptureunion.org (USA)
www.su.org.au (Australia)

Contents

Contents

Contents

The Easter message is at the heart of the Christian faith. It is something we want to share with others and to know and understand more fully ourselves.

More Easter Cracked is a compilation of great ideas for getting the message into people's hearts and minds at this important time of year. It focuses on the events of Jesus' life in the week before he died, on his death and burial and on the resurrection appearances. There are always new things to discover as we think about these stories and new challenges to face as we grow older.

Since we are all different, leaders need various ways of engaging people in the amazing truths presented in the Gospel accounts – we don't all learn and respond in the same way! And, of course, what a child of three needs to know about why Jesus died is different from what an adult can take in. For these reasons, *More Easter Cracked* is brimful of different approaches – drama, stories, games, craft activities, illustrated talks, songs, rhymes and ideas for events – all tailored for various age-groupings, including for times when all ages are learning and worshipping together.

You may wish to use some items just as they are to fit into your Easter programme. Alternatively, you may want to create your own events and services, taking ideas from different sections of the resource, according to the needs of your group or congregation. Perhaps some of the ideas will spark off your own creativity so that you will create your own, tailor-made events!

Whatever you do, have fun! The Easter season brings some very sombre and serious themes to Christians and to those we want to reach. On the other hand, there is room and opportunity for enjoyment, warmth and celebration. I hope that you will enjoy using this resource; that you will be encouraged to try out new ideas and to make Easter-time memorable for those you are leading and for yourself.

Our thanks to all those who have contributed to this book through their writing for the *Light* series: *Light Years*, *theGRID*, *Xstream*, *Splash!* and *Bubbles*.

Christine Wright

Introduction

Suppers for Maundy Thursday

Reflections on the Last Supper with a simple meal

Ideally, these events take place in the run-up to Easter, preferably on Maundy Thursday and in the evening. It is a gathering with a sense of intimacy with a simple meal to share – perhaps bread, cheese, grapes and a hot drink, all sitting around a table or arrangement of tables. After the meal, but before the clutter of the meal has been cleared away, the script is read where they sit by volunteers, male and female, who have been eating. The aim is to recreate the atmosphere of the last supper Jesus shared with his friends before he died, and it is ideal to share in an informal celebration of Holy Communion around the table immediately afterwards.

It was a dark night

This script imagines Jesus' disciples reflecting, some years later, on their experiences during the Last Supper.

Leader: It was a dark night – and they had crept to that upper room to celebrate Passover together in secret with Jesus. The disciples are together again, perhaps a few years later, and reflect on that life-changing night. The upper room had been a place of safety in a world of violence and danger, but even as they sat around the table, the betrayer sat among them. Some had taken swords, ready to defend themselves and kill if necessary – for they hoped the crisis had come and he would soon declare his intention to conquer the hated Romans and set up his kingdom. Some, despite everything Jesus had taught them, cherished ambitions of greatness in his kingdom. Yet all would reject Jesus before the night was out.

Reader 1: We were scared. The Jewish authorities were out to get Jesus. That's why we had to meet in secret to celebrate Passover.

Reader 2: Only a few weeks before there had been a riot against the Romans. Someone had been murdered and Barabbas had been arrested for it. Everyone expected him to be executed in the next few days.

Reader 1: The authorities had been watching Jesus very carefully, hoping he'd slip up and give them an excuse to arrest him too. There were spies everywhere.

Reader 2: When Jesus sent us to get the Passover ready, we had to find the upper room without being noticed. We felt as though the whole of Jerusalem was on the edge of a knife.

Reader 3: The Lord washed our feet that night. When we arrived in the upper room where we were to eat Passover, we were tired and foot-sore. The touch of his hands was as refreshing as the water. We felt that we had been made clean through and through, inside and outside.

Reader 4: All the more because he was our Lord. It was not his role to wash our feet, but he did – gently and lovingly. He didn't make us feel guilty that none of us had thought to do that menial task.

Reader 3: He made the point, I think...

Reader 4: In view of the argument we'd been having that night.

Reader 5: We had been arguing about who was the greatest. It seemed important at the time. If the time was coming when Jesus would need generals, tacticians and chief ministers, we wanted to make sure that everyone had the pecking order clear.

Reader 6: I saw myself as his right-hand man and wanted to remind the others of how Jesus had relied on me. In difficult moments I had been the one who had stood beside him ready to fight if necessary.

Reader 5: But *I* was his confidante. He'd taken me with him and showed me things he'd never shown the others and discussed matters of real importance with me.

Reader 6: That attitude made me angry. I thought that my strength of will and body were what were going to matter in the days ahead.

Reader 7: He told us to buy swords. He said we should sell everything we had, even our cloaks, to buy a sword.

Reader 8: He must have known about the violent days ahead – when they'd try to kill us because we belonged to him.

Reader 7: How could we have known then what it would mean to walk the way of peace in a violent world, not with a real sword, but with the sword of the Spirit, the word of God?

Reader 8: The threat of persecution was so far from our thoughts then. How real it became in just a few short months.

Reader 9: He told me that I would be tested like a farmer separating the wheat from the chaff. I knew the hard threshing and winnowing that night when I found I lacked the courage to stand up for him.

Reader 10: We all ran away: every single one of us. Faced with the threat of violence, we all took to our heels and nobody stood beside him when they seized him. And no one spoke up for him.

Reader 9: I thought I would. I told him I'd never let him down even if I was sent to jail or even if I was to die with him. But when I saw him being arrested and faced the reality of jail and death, I denied I'd ever known him.

Reader 10: If he'd told us to fight, we might have made a stand, but he stopped us. We couldn't respond as he did. We couldn't match his calm acceptance that his time had come.

Reader 11: He even knew that one of us would betray him. In Judas' mind the deed had already been done. He'd sold himself to the religious authorities for thirty pieces of silver. His heart was dark and cold. His love for Jesus had died and turned to dust. Knowing what the chief priests were capable of, he promised to turn Jesus over to them. With that knowledge in his head, he sat at table sharing the Passover meal, planning to slip out and bring the rabble to arrest him.

Reader 1: Jesus knew that we were scared. Because he loved us he showed us his courage.

Reader 2: And he showed us his love to the end.

Reader 3: Jesus knew we were in need of healing and cleansing. Because he loved us he poured himself out for us.

Reader 4: And he showed us his love to the end.

Reader 5: Jesus knew that we were overambitious and proud. Because he loved us he showed us his humility.

Reader 6: And he showed us his love to the end.

Reader 7: He knew that his followers would not always live in peace and security. Because he loved us, he promised that he would never leave us.

Reader 8: And he showed us his love to the end.

Reader 9: He knew that we would let him down, however good our intentions. Because he loved us, he remained true to us even though it cost him his life.

Reader 10: And he showed us his love to the end.

Reader 11: Jesus knew the betrayer was there with us, but still he loved him. He uncovered the evil in us all: the betrayer, the denier, the coward, the over-confident, the proud, the boastful, the treacherous and the mean-spirited. We couldn't accept the truth then, not openly anyway. But the truth is that he was the only one in that room who was innocent. And he showed us his love to the end.

Bible Reading: Luke 22:1–39

Leader: It is dark tonight, too. As we meet around the table, remembering how Jesus gave his body and blood for us, he uncovers the evil in us all. (*Pause.*) We are truly sorry that we let him down and come to him now in repentance and faith. (*Pause.*) And we remember that Jesus also reveals to us the depth of his love. With his disciples so long ago we rejoice that his death has made us whole again and that his love remains with us to the end.

Suggested song 'My Lord, what love is this?' *SOF 398*

What is he carrying?

For this script you will need the following items: a picture of a small child or baby, a clod of earth in a small bowl, a coin, a few strands of rope tied together, a bowl of water with a small towel. You will need several of each item, depending on the size of the group, so that everyone can see one of each item. Alongside each item you will need a lighted candle (tea light). Explain before you begin that when each item is mentioned someone should pick it up and pass it around those sitting near them so that everyone has a chance to hold it while the reader is speaking. When everyone has done so, it should be replaced beside the lighted candle. Ask people to extinguish the candles when they are prompted to do so. Reader 1 should also have a piece of bread and a cup of wine to pick up when they are mentioned.

Reader 1: Imagine you are there. It is night and

you are meeting in secret. The room has been prepared and, as you come in and shake back the hood you are wearing and ease out of your cloak, the lamps are being lit around the room. There is a table on which a meal is being placed. You stand at one side while the others come in and begin to take their places at the table. Jesus comes in last and shuts the door. He stands looking at his friends – at you – and he looks sad. He knows this is the last time he will eat with you all. He knows the danger outside in the dark streets and he knows the danger inside the room. And yet his heart is filled with love and compassion.

Reader 2: It was now the day before the Passover festival. Jesus knew that the hour had come for him to leave the world and go to the Father. He had always loved those in the world who were his own, and he loved them to the very end.

Reader 1: But as yet Jesus does not take his place at the table. Instead he stands thinking, his eyes looking at each of his friends in turn. He is carrying a concern for them all. He wants to demonstrate his love. You take your place among your friends as they begin to discuss what Jesus is doing.

Reader 2: What is he carrying now?

Reader 3: I remember when he carried a child. How gently he lifted the baby from her mother's arms! We had been arguing about which of us was greatest. Some said that they were the strongest; some said they had a better education; some said they were the wisest; some said they were closer to Jesus.

But Jesus took a baby and showed her around the circle of us and told us that if we wanted to be great, we'd have to shape up and become just like this little child.

And he lit a lamp in our minds. We saw that greatness is not about wielding authority, but about accepting littleness. Greatness is being willing to take the lowest place.

He lit a lamp and we saw a glimpse of a kingdom where the little ones are the leaders and where those willing to be thought inferior are the greatest in God's eyes.

Reader 2: What is he carrying now?

Reader 4: I remember when he took the dust of the ground and made mud with his spittle. He carried it to a blind man's eyes – mud to be washed away, dirt to be removed. Oh the light that streamed into that man's eyes! He washed the mud away and he could see!

And we began to see too. He lit a lamp in our minds. We saw that this world's darkness could be removed. The dirt that sticks to everything we try to do could be washed away. The light is revealed. And the light could take away the menace of darkness.

And then Jesus said, 'I am the light of the world.' We saw that we did not have to go looking for the light. The light had come to us in Jesus. We only had to stay close to him to have the light of life. He lit a lamp and we saw a glimpse of a kingdom where we would walk in safety through life. No more darkness – just the light of Jesus.

Reader 2: What is he carrying now?

Reader 5: I remember when he carried a coin. He took it in his hand and turned it over thoughtfully, considering the inscriptions on both sides, considering the question, 'Is it against our Law to pay taxes to the Roman Emperor or not?'

God or the Emperor? The question jangled in our minds, knowing that it was a trap. How could he get out of this one? Whichever answer he gave, he would be in the wrong. If he said: 'The Law does not allow us to pay taxes to Rome', would they make him out to be a rebel against the Emperor? If he said: 'The Law does allow us to pay taxes to Rome', would this be taken as a sign that he was a rebel against God?

He was carrying the question in his mind, just as he was carrying the coin in his hand. Rome or God? The secular or the sacred? One or the other...?

Then he lit a lamp in our minds. 'Pay the Emperor what belongs to the Emperor and pay God what belongs to God.' How simple, how neat, how revolutionary! He lit a lamp and we saw a glimpse of his kingdom where there is no secular and sacred, but one seamless order in which God is supreme – a kingdom where God is working alongside our human attempts to order society. God is in government. God is in politics.

Reader 2: What is he carrying now?

Reader 6: I remember that he carried a rope whip and drove out the animals being sold for sacrifice. And he turned out those who were making an unfair profit. How surprised we were! He had always seemed so peaceful, dealing gently with the weak. He was only angry with the hypocrites who taught others what they did not practise themselves.

That day, he took startling, alarming action – even more alarming since he did so in the place of prayer. He made a whip and carried it to mete out justice. He carried it to rout out thievery. He carried it to expose irreverence for the holy God.

And he lit a lamp in our minds. We saw that devotion to God was not about having the right coins or the perfect animal sacrifices. He lit a lamp in our minds and gave us a glimpse of a kingdom where worship of God can be straightforward, direct, honest and sincere.

Reader 2: What is he carrying now? Now he is carrying a bowl of water and a towel. Look, he has put the servant's apron around his own waist. He is kneeling down to wash our feet. Why would he do the work of a servant, this one who is greater than us all? And yet he kneels humbly, washing, drying, kissing our feet with his gentle touch.

He is lighting a lamp in our minds. He is showing us majesty at the disposal of the mean; he is showing us the glory of God poured out for the wretched; he is showing us the powerful serving the powerless. He has lit a lamp and given us a glimpse of a kingdom where entry is not deserved or achieved. It is by grace – by being washed.

Reader 1: And now Jesus takes his place at the table and the meal is eaten. It is quiet. There is much to think about, but little to say. The darkness seems to press in on everyone.

Reader 2: What is he carrying now? He has taken a piece of bread and a cup of wine. He is speaking about the unthinkable. He is speaking about his death. He is plunging us into darkness. What of the light he has given us? If he dies, the lights are extinguished and our minds are left in darkness. *(A candle is extinguished.)*

Lord, have mercy on us.
Reader 3: He carried a child. If Jesus is not with us, we must live in a world that rejects littleness and where the strong seizes power. They will injure him and kill him. The light will be snuffed out. *(A candle is extinguished.)*
Lord, have mercy on us.

Reader 4: He carried a clod of mud. If he is not with us, we must live without the light. The dangers of darkness will overcome us. The light will be snuffed out. *(A candle is extinguished.)*
Lord, have mercy on us.

Reader 5: He carried a coin. If he is not with us, we are at the mercy of a political system in which God has no place. The light will be snuffed out. *(A candle is extinguished.)*
Lord, have mercy on us.

Reader 6: He carried a rope whip. If he is not with us, we must try to please God with our religious observance. We must bring sacrifices to appease his anger. The light will be snuffed out. *(A candle is extinguished.)*
Lord, have mercy on us.

Reader 2: He carried a bowl of water and a towel. If he is not with us, how can we be clean? How can we be forgiven? The light will be snuffed out. *(A candle is extinguished.)*
Lord, have mercy on us.

Reader 1: But Jesus is carrying bread and wine – his own body and blood. Let us wait, with bated breath, to see what he says.

Bible reading: Luke 22:14–20

Sing an appropriate song or hymn before leading into a celebration of Holy Communion.

Other ideas for Easter events

The last meal
A token meal with a meaning for older children, young people and adults

Beforehand prepare some charoset (peeled, cored and chopped apples, cinnamon, a little sugar, honey and sweet red wine or grape juice), horseradish sauce, red grape juice, matzos or other flat bread, paper cups. Set out the food on a table which everyone can sit around. Pour everyone some grape juice, but ask people not to drink it yet.

Explain that you are going to use the food on the table to help you to pray and reflect on Jesus' death and what it means to us. Read these words and perform the actions in italics:

As we take and break the unleavened bread, we remember that Jesus was broken because of us, because of the things we have done wrong. (*Take a matzo and break it, and invite everyone else to do the same.*)

As we taste the bitter herbs, we remember the things we have done wrong. We remember that our sin makes God sad. (*Take half of your matzo, dip it in the horseradish and eat it. Invite everyone else to do the same.*)

As we taste the sweet charoset, we remember that God wants to set us free from our lives of sin. (*Take the other half of your matzo and dip it in the charoset and eat it, encouraging everyone else to do the same.*)

As we drink the juice of the grape, we remember that Jesus' blood has rescued us from death. (*Drink some juice and invite everyone else to do the same.*)

Pray: 'We thank you, God, for the story of your people. We thank you that we are part of that story. We thank you that you sent Jesus to be one of us, to find us and to save us by his death on the cross. We thank you for his resurrection and the promise of new life it brings to us all. Amen.'

Walk through the week
Ideas for an event to explain the events of the week before Jesus died

Arrange an event or display to enable everyone to understand more fully the events of the last week of Jesus' life, from Palm Sunday through to the crucifixion and resurrection.

At its simplest this could be a showing of the complete film of *The Miracle Maker*, the puppet version of the gospel story that will appeal to all ages. Alternatively, arrange a series of still-life displays illustrating the events of holy week, for example: Palm Sunday (cloaks and palm branches laid on the ground); the Last Supper (a table laid with bread and wine); Judas' betrayal (a bag spilling out silver coins); the arrest and trials (crown of thorns, purple robe and whip); the crucifixion (a cross). Open the displays to the community and arrange a time for them to be available. Encourage people to spend time reflecting on each one.

Mix and match
Ideas for a family event for Easter

Search this book for ideas and put together a special event for children and their families. You could include different ways of praying, games, stories and food ideas. The event could take place alongside a lunch after church, or a special Easter Saturday perhaps the following week. You could use some of the recipes for chocolate decorations and have an egg-decorating competition – you could even make it a timed 'chef challenge' judged by everyone else. There are also a number of ideas for traditional Easter games, such as egg rolling. As many of the ideas are self-explanatory, they are ideal for different groups in the church to take their turn to organise for a special family fun day to celebrate Easter. Put into any search engine the phrase 'Easter traditional games children decorations' and see what pops up!

Come fishing!
An outreach fish supper with invitation to copy

Share the good news that Jesus is alive by holding a fish supper. You could get children to plan the supper so they can share the Easter story with their family and friends. Include the story of the breakfast on the beach (John 21:1–19) to make the link to the fish supper! The children should think of whom they will invite and how they are going to present the story to them – perhaps in drama or a Bible reading with mime. While some children plan this, others could make invitations and decorations, and plan where to get the fish and chips from. You could create your own publicity and/or use the invitations on page 12. Arrange a time and place for the event to happen, and ask God to show himself to the people who are invited!

Easter events

Dear _____

You are invited
to an Easter fish
and chip supper

On: _____

At: _____ (place)

At: _____ (time)

Please come and celebrate
Easter with us!

Dear _____

You are invited
to an Easter fish
and chip supper

On: _____

At: _____ (place)

At: _____ (time)

Please come and celebrate
Easter with us!

Short talks for all ages

What kind of king?
An all-age talk for Palm Sunday

You will need: improvised items fit for a king or queen (or large pictures of them) – robe, sceptre, grand transport, red carpet, loyal servant, costly gift, grand tombstone; items fit for Jesus – donkey (toy or picture), old coats, plain bowl, pitta bread, plain goblet or cup

Ask a volunteer to be a king or queen sitting on a throne. Dress them in a 'rich' robe and give them a sceptre. Surround them with the following items explaining why each is appropriate to royalty: transport, for example a toy Rolls Royce; a red carpet; loyal servants kneeling around; someone bringing a costly gift; a grand royal tombstone (for when they die).

Explain that as Jesus arrived in Jerusalem he was cheered as a king. By riding a donkey he would have reminded the people of Zechariah 9:9 which said that one day Jerusalem's king would come in this way. But what sort of a king was Jesus going to be?

Step by step remove the items from your volunteer, replacing them with others as follows. As you do so, talk about the events of Jesus' arrival in Jerusalem and of the Last Supper.

1 Remove your king's robe and sceptre. Jesus was not rich but poor.

2 Replace the Rolls Royce with a donkey. Jesus' transport was not impressive to show his power. A donkey was lowly and humble (Mark 11:2).

3 Replace the red carpet with old coats. Jesus didn't get an official welcome from important leaders but was cheered by the crowds travelling to Jerusalem (11:8).

4 Take away the loyal servants and leave a plain bowl at his feet. Later that week Jesus shared a meal with his followers. Soon they would all leave him. Jesus said one who dipped his bread in the same bowl would even betray him (14:18).

5 Replace the costly gift with pitta bread. Jesus did not receive gifts from his followers at that meal; instead he broke bread and gave it to them as a sign that he was giving everything to them – even his own life as he would die on the cross (14:22).

6 Replace the tombstone with a cup or goblet. Jesus did not need a grand royal tomb (like the pyramids). He would not be dead for long. He shared a cup with his followers as a sign of a new promise from God.

He said he himself would be alive again to drink it in God's kingdom. It was a promise of new life for us with him for ever (14:24,25).

These elements of the talk could be split in two – after the reading of Mark 11:1-11 (items 1-3) and of Mark 14:12-26 (items 4-6).

Breaking bread
A brief talk with a demonstration suitable as part of Holy Communion

You will need: appropriate music, a long loaf or baguette cut almost completely through lengthways, a nail or peg, a glass of wine or grape juice (optional)

Explain that at the Last Supper, on the night before he died, Jesus broke bread and referred to his broken body. Jesus was prepared for what was to come – he knew it to be all part of God's plan. Perhaps the disciples at Emmaus remembered this when they recognised him as he broke the bread.

Over some quiet, ambient music, or perhaps whilst the congregation sing a suitable song such as 'Broken for me', complete the breaking of the bread. Take the two pieces and pin them together to make the shape of a cross.

You may want to teach this refrain for use in Communion services, or to say together now as you hold up a communion cup containing wine and break off a piece of the bread:

Leader: We break bread together
All: To remind us of Jesus.
Leader: We share a cup of wine
All: To remind us of Jesus.

Extending my life
An all-age talk with drama and music suitable for Easter Day

You will need: recruit beforehand three volunteers prepared to mime the actions listed below, (optional) music CD 'Live forever' by Oasis from the album *Definitely Maybe* (1994)

The three volunteers come forward, one by one, and each mimes one of the actions below. Ask each one what they are doing. They should reply as follows:

1 (*Eating a banana.*) 'I'm extending my life by eating a healthy diet.'

2 (*Filling in a form.*) 'I'm extending my life by using private medical insurance.'

3 (*Wearing training kit, begins jogging and stretching exercises.*) 'I'm extending my life by using a sound exercise regime.'

Say: 'We all love to find ways to live a little longer even though we know that our bodies won't last for ever. Because of Jesus' resurrection we have been given the hope that we can live with God for ever. The message of Easter is that we can live beyond death; live for ever, because of what Jesus did for us on the cross.

At this point you may like to play the CD track 'Live Forever' by Oasis from the album *Definitely Maybe* (1994), or you could do the introductory activity while the track is being played.

Unbelievable?

An Easter Day activity and talk for all ages together

You will need: paper, pens

Ask the congregation to get into mixed-age groups of no more than ten people. Give each group a sheet of paper and a pen and explain that you want them to imagine they are back at school and have forgotten to complete their homework. Not wanting to admit this to the teacher, they should compose a short note that 'explains' why they haven't completed their homework, aiming to make it as convincing as possible. As soon as everyone has started, quickly go over to one of the groups and quietly tell them to do their best to make their note unbelievable (for example, tales of aliens coming down and taking the homework away with them).

When everyone has finished, select a few groups to read out their 'notes to the teacher' and invite feedback from the rest of the congregation as regards how convincing the notes are. The group with the special instruction should be the last group to read out their note. Hopefully they will have followed the instruction sufficiently well as to draw gasps and giggles from the rest

of the congregation. The idea is that everyone should agree that this note describes something impossible and therefore unbelievable.

Lead on from this to talk about how Mark 16:1–8 contains the incredible statement that Jesus was raised to life after being crucified. There's no denying that it is a remarkable claim. Because of this, some people refuse to believe it. They suggest that it was simply made up by his friends to try and fool people into believing that his and their hopes and dreams didn't all come to a sad end on the cross. The reaction of the women in Mark's account of the resurrection confirms that the claim that Jesus came back to life is not an easy thing to believe.

However, the note-writing activity has illustrated that if someone is making up something in the hope that people will believe it, they don't include details that are hard to believe! When Mark wrote his Gospel, he knew that those who read it might find the claim that Jesus came back to life difficult to believe – so why did he include it if he wanted people to believe what he was writing and take it seriously? We must assume that he included such an unbelievable claim because he had no choice – that's what happened! However hard it might be to take in, that's what happened! The power of God raised Jesus back to life after he had died on the cross.

Faced with being the first to hear of such a demonstration of God's power, is it any wonder that the women who went to the tomb were initially left speechless (v 8)? We know from the other Gospel accounts, however, that the women did eventually pass on this astonishing news that they could hardly take in, and it was then passed from person to person and recorded by Matthew, Mark, Luke and John in their accounts of Jesus' life. Though we might at first tremble and be confused by the news of Jesus coming back to life, we can move into celebration when we realise that it must be true!

Empty egg

An introductory talk for Easter Day for children or all ages together

You will need: A blown egg with a Bible verse clue inside

Beforehand, prepare an egg by using a darning needle to make a small hole at the top and bottom. Slightly enlarge one of the holes, then swirl the needle around to break up the yolk. Blow through the smallest hole so that the egg runs into a bowl. Wash out the egg in warm water. Write the words of Luke 9:22 on a slip of paper. Roll it up and push it into the egg.

Holding the egg so your fingers cover the holes, ask the children to guess whether it's hard-boiled or raw. Break it over a bowl and enjoy their surprise. The women were even more surprised when they found the tomb empty. Read or ask someone to read the slip of paper (Luke 9:22). Say that Jesus had given several clues that he would rise again.

Dead and buried?

A 'God slot' script for young people and adults

Possibly the most famous Egyptian pharaoh is Tutankhamun. This boy king died in his late teens and remained at rest in Egypt's Valley of the Kings for more than 3,300 years. That's almost as old as [insert one of your leader's names here].

All that changed in November 1922, when Howard Carter, who was excavating in the area, discovered Tutankhamun's tomb. The tomb almost escaped discovery and could have been undiscovered to this day. Carter had been searching for the tomb for a number of years for his financial supporter Lord Carnarvon. Carnarvon had decided that enough time and money had been spent on the mission with little return. However, Carter managed to persuade Carnarvon to fund one more season and, within days of resuming, the tomb was found.

It contained four gilded shrines nested one inside the other. The innermost of these covered a stone sarcophagus. Inside were three coffins, the innermost made of 110 kilograms of solid gold. Inside this coffin lay the pharaoh himself, wearing the famous gold mask.

Carter concluded that the tomb had been broken into on two occasions soon after the pharaoh was buried. After each break-in, officials of the necropolis resealed the tomb. Fortunately, the tomb robbers did not get away with very much, and the material sealed in with Tutankhamun may now be viewed in Cairo's Egyptian Museum with a few items in the Luxor Museum.

Finding the tomb was a big shock. Finding it

full of gold and the Pharaoh was an even bigger shock, as many of the Egyptian tombs had been robbed over the centuries.

After Jesus had been killed and buried, three of his followers had a big shock when they went to his tomb. They didn't find treasure and a dead king – they found that Jesus was no longer dead, but alive. Now, that was a shock! And an even bigger shock is that Jesus is still alive and wants to be our friend.

How can you be so sure?

Considering the evidence for the resurrection for young people and adults

Hi, my name is [insert your own name] and I know that Jesus is alive. 'Ah!' I hear you say, 'How can you be so sure?' Well, it's true I haven't actually seen Jesus in person to touch and so on, like the two Marys when they went to his tomb. But a few years ago... [include your own testimony]. Well, I haven't looked back.

But maybe you're not sure what all this is about. I mean, how can someone who was dead, be alive? Perhaps he wasn't dead in the first place? Well, that's a little far-fetched – if you believe that, you'd believe anything. After all, the Romans were very efficient; they knew when someone was dead, and they were experts in crucifixion, which was how they killed Jesus.

Or perhaps the women were lying – they made up this story; they didn't really see Jesus. Yeah, that's a good point, but women were not trusted at the time these events took place. If you went to court, the testimony of a woman wasn't allowed! Now, if you wanted to say that Jesus had risen from the dead, the last people you would say saw him would be a couple of women! But the writers of the New Testament wanted everyone to know it, because it was true. And then, after the women had seen Jesus, others saw him too, including the rest of the disciples.

So if you want to know more, there's always someone who can help. (Explain who to contact if anyone wants to find out more.)

A disciple's tale

A monologue in the style of Friends, *the American sitcom of the 1990s*

You will need: a prepared actor, *Friends* theme music: 'I'll be there for you' by The Rembrandts (optional)

The following script retells the Bible text from an unusual point of view. It uses words, ideas and characters from the US TV sitcom *Friends*. Introduce it with the *Friends* theme music.

Script:
A disciple called Chandler

Well, no one told me it was meant to be this way: my job's a joke, I'm broke, my worship life's DOA; if it had been invented yet I'd be stuck in second gear; it hasn't been my day, my week, my month or even my year.

It all started so well, the following-Jesus business. He did the water-into-wine thing, the healing thing, the multiplying-food thing (Joey loved that one) and we did the following-him thing. Trouble is, we had to follow him all the way into Jerusalem, right the way into an argument and ultimately to the foot of the cross without a coffee stop. That was so not the way it was meant to work out. It's not easy just to bury three years of your life and go back to work, or foosball.

So we were sitting there talking about what had happened. Monica tidied up, Phoebe wrote a song about it, Rachel bought some shoes and Ross explained what would happen to Jesus' bones over the next 20,000 years. Joey ate muffins. Which was when *he* came in. 'Hey!' he said. It's scary when dead people talk to you, so we didn't say 'Hey!' back. We just stared and wondered if he was real.

'Go on, touch,' he said. 'I'm totally cool about you touching me. It won't hurt. Hey, are those muffins?'

'Get lost,' said Joey, attending at last. 'Dead people don't eat.' 'I do,' said Jesus, taking a muffin. 'Hey, these are good – better than fish.'

And sitting there once again, like old times, he told us that what had happened to him had been prophesied. And he explained how he had to do the rising-from-the-dead thing and we had to do the telling-everyone-the-good-news thing. You may have thought Jesus had come to an end; but he's still on every night.

Palm Sunday drama

Dramatic action to accompany a Bible reading of Mark 11:1–10 for all ages together

You will need: 6 to 12 people who have practised assembling the two frozen scenes

The 'actors' assemble a frozen scene showing Jesus riding through the crowds. At the same time Mark 11:1–10 is read. Begin with Jesus seated on a tall stool holding imaginary reins. During the reading, the actors add themselves one by one to the scene – as Jesus' disciples, helping or following behind him, and as the crowds – cheering, laying down coats, some puzzled or disapproving. Practise the timing so that the scene reaches completion just before the reading ends.

As the actors briefly hold the scene, invite the congregation to imagine themselves as part of that scene. Where would they put themselves? A few people could give their answers aloud.

Create a second scene with the same actors as Mark 14:17–25 is read. Show the moment in Mark 14:23 as Jesus holds out the cup to a disciple. The disciples should show a range of reactions – excited, sad, confused and angry.

Again, hold the scene and invite the congregation to imagine where they would put themselves in it. How would they be reacting to Jesus' words?

An extraordinary event

An account of the resurrection in the style of a chat show

Scene: TV chat show
Characters: Mary Magdalene, Other Mary, Lavina McCool

Lavina: Welcome, everyone, to this week's show. We are privileged to have two ladies with us today, with an extraordinary story to tell. Please welcome Mary Magdalene and her friend, also called Mary. (*Everyone claps.*) Mary M, is it OK if I call you that? (*Mary M nods.*) Now tell us about your extraordinary event.

Mary M: Well, Mary and I *(looks at other Mary)* went to the place where they had buried Jesus after he'd been crucified. When we got there we had the shock of our lives, didn't we, Mary? *(Other Mary nods.)* You see, when we got there, there was this sort of earthquake. We were terrified, weren't we, Mary? *(Other Mary nods again.)* And then, you'll never believe this, Lavina, we saw a real angel! All shiny and white, wasn't he, Mary? *(Other Mary nods.)* The angel rolled the stone away from the tomb where Jesus was, the guards collapsed in a heap on the ground in shock, and we just stood transfixed in amazement, fear and... *(Other Mary cuts in.)*

Other Mary: Joy!

Lavina: *(To Other Mary.)* You say 'joy', Mary? Why was that?

Other Mary: Well, this angel told us that Jesus was alive; he had risen from the dead! And then the next thing we knew he was there, talking to us, alive and kicking, as they say!

Lavina: You mean Jesus actually spoke to you both?! *(Looks at both Marys.)*

Mary M: That's it! Can you imagine how we felt, Lavina? Jesus spoke to us, a real, live, living, speaking Jesus! *(Other Mary nods enthusiastically.)*

Lavina: Well, thank you both for sharing that truly amazing extraordinary event with us. *(To viewers.)* And join us next week when we will be meeting a guy called Thomas, who claims to have touched Jesus after he rose from the dead. We look forward to hearing about this extraordinary event. Goodnight and God bless.

Bible interview

An improvised drama for three actors in the form of a chat show suitable for Easter Day

You will need: three prepared actors dressed as two disciples and a 'chat show' host, a sofa and any other props to mimic a breakfast-TV-type programme

The actors playing the disciples should make themselves very familiar with Luke 24:13-35.

Welcome the audience and viewers to the show, and then welcome the two disciples at the front. The host should interview them briefly about

their experience on the road to Emmaus. Make sure they stick to the main points:

We saw Jesus die.
We know he was buried.
We were walking back disconsolate.
We met a man who told us what Jesus' death meant, using scriptures such as Isaiah 53 as a starting point.
When that man came into our house and ate with us, we recognised him as he broke the bread. We can't say why we didn't recognise him before. As soon as we recognised him he vanished, and we went all the way back to Jerusalem again to tell the others. They said they'd had a similar experience.

As a conclusion emphasise that God's plan for Jesus to rise from death was fulfilled. Our Bibles are the record of many interviews with witnesses who testify to this.

Jesus appears to his followers

A dramatisation of Luke 24:36-49 with a drama challenge for young people or adults

The script below is a dramatisation of Luke 24:36-49 which can be used as it is in place of reading it from the Bible. You could follow the dramatisation by challenging small groups to create their own drama based on the Bible passage. Give out Bibles and encourage the group to work with the Bible text. When you have finished, perform the drama (to other groups, if possible).

Cast: Jesus, the disciples and some women

Jesus: *(Standing in the midst of the group assembled.)* Peace be with you.

Disciple 1: He can't be real; it's a ghost! *(The other disciples look afraid.)*

Jesus: What's the matter? I am real. Come and see my hands and feet. Touch me. I am not a ghost because I am a living body!

Disciple 2: *(Touching Jesus.)* Wow! That is amazing! He is real!

Jesus: Do you have any food I could have?

Disciple 3: We have some fish. *(He gives Jesus some fish. Jesus eats it.)*

Jesus: Do you remember when I was with you before? I said that everything written about me must happen. (*Disciples all nod in agreement.*)

Jesus: Well, it was written that I would suffer and rise from the dead on the third day. It was also written that people's hearts and lives would be changed and that they would receive forgiveness in my name. This message is given to you, for all nations, starting in Jerusalem. You are to go and tell others, in my name, this good news, and I will send the Holy Spirit to help you.

Fish to go

A monologue based on Luke 24:36–49

You will need: a copy of a phone directory, a mobile phone

(*Peter is sitting at a table looking through the phone directory. He has a phone with him.*)

Peter: (*Muttering.*) Fish and chip shops. Fish and chip shops. Aaaahhh! Here we are. Now which one to choose? 'The Jolly Frier' or 'The Tasty Plaice' or 'The Codfather'.

(*Looks up suddenly and sees audience.*) Hello. My name's Peter. Never used to have to buy my fish. Fishing was my game, but all that changed when I started to follow Jesus and became one of his disciples. I listened to him; I learned from him. (*Thoughtfully.*) Then I watched him die. Horrible it was... (*Animatedly.*) Then that changed too! Let me tell you about that Sunday evening, in a room upstairs...

We were all together when Jesus just appeared among us and greeted us with the words, 'Peace be with you.'

Holy mackerel, I thought. Dead men don't talk! Dead men don't walk! Peace? You must be joking! We were terrified! We thought he was a ghost... Well, we had no other explanation for it. You wouldn't have had either. We looked at his hands and feet. He invited us to touch him. We could hardly believe it. When someone you love dies, you long to see them again. We were amazed and glad and confused and terrified all at once! What happened next changed our lives. Jesus ate some fish! Dead men don't eat fish! I'd seen him do some stuff – but this! Fish was there one minute, munched the next! Proof. No doubt about it. Saw it with my own eyes.

Then he explained the Old Testament to us. He pointed to places where the prophets clearly say that the Messiah must suffer and die and come back to life three days later. Then, Jesus gave us all a new job to do. We had to go and tell people about Jesus all over the world. Be a fisher of men in a global pond! Who'd have thought it? Not me. There are people spreading the good news of Jesus all over the place now! Jesus gave us the equipment for the job too – power from heaven: God's Holy Spirit. Can't say fairer than that, can you?

Oops! Sorry, got to go. (*Dials a number and speaks into phone.*) Hello. Yes, fish to go please.

Easter story drama

A simple Bible story drama for young children

This drama will help very young children enter into the Easter story by using their whole bodies. Teach the children the actions to the mime below. Ask them to begin by lying on the floor in a space so that they have plenty of room to move.

Jesus' body was put into the cave (*Lie on the floor.*)
The stone was rolled in front of the cave (*Curl up in a ball.*)
But when Jesus' friends came, the stone had rolled away. (*Roll to one side.*)
They were very sad. (*Sit up with a sad face.*)
Then they heard a voice.
They looked up. Who was it? (*Look up.*)
They looked closer. Who was it? (*Stand up.*)
Then Jesus said, 'It's me.'
They jumped for joy (*jump up and down*) and ran to tell all Jesus' friends: (*Run across the room.*)
'Jesus is alive!' (*Clap and cheer.*)

An evening with Jesus

A meditation on John 13:1-14

Encourage everyone to sit comfortably, to close their eyes if they wish and imagine their way into the scene as you slowly read the following:

It has been a long, hot day.

At last you are getting ready to sit down and share the Passover celebration meal with Jesus and the other disciples. It has all been a bit strange recently. Jesus has been talking about some weird stuff. You don't understand it all, but you hope that it will eventually start making sense. It is certainly nice to be sitting here with friends, about to eat.

You think back to what Jesus has been saying. You know he is special, and deep down you're pretty sure that he is the great leader you have been waiting for – the Messiah, God's anointed special person. And if that is so, he will be the greatest king and leader Israel has ever known. But today things have been a little odd – he seems to be talking about dying, of falling down, of going away – but at the same time, he is saying that this is necessary. Totally weird! But hey! That is the way he talks at times. You don't always understand his words; you know you should, and they sound really deep, but they sometimes don't make sense.

Anyway, dinner should be here soon. That will make things a little easier – some food after the long, hot and busy day you've had.

Then Jesus appears with a bowl and towel. What is he doing?! He kneels before you and, removing your sandals, begins to wash your feet – your hot, sticky, dusty feet. It has been a particularly hot day, and with all the walking, your feet are really quite whiffy.

This great man, this future king, the person who is going to make your country great again, is here kneeling and washing your feet – doing a servant's job. You are lost for words.

Peter isn't though. Is he ever? He asks that if he needs to be washed, Jesus should wash his whole body. Peter always does go over the top. But as always Jesus simply smiles – that look of love, concern, pity and joy that's always there – and tells Peter he doesn't need to be washed; he is already clean.

Then off he goes again talking about dying, and we're all going to run away apparently. I laugh as Peter again speaks up, but Jesus stops Peter in his tracks. Peter's confidence goes, the blood drains from his face, and I see a tear in his eye as Jesus tells him that, before the next day, Peter will say he doesn't even know Jesus.

It's been a long, hot day.

Jesus, the table-turner

A meditation based on the events of Matthew 21:12,13

You will need: A small robust table

To begin, remind the group that Jesus wanted to free people from what was getting in the way of their relationship with God. We still allow things to get in the way – for example, past sins, hurts or an inability to forgive. It could be a misconception of God – for example, 'He could never forgive me'. It could be regularly repeating sins or even simply going through the motions rather than developing our relationship with God. Without any pressure, encourage everyone to think of things in their lives that get in between them and God.

Ask everyone to close their eyes and quietly reflect on their life and their relationship with God. Suggest that they ask God to show them things in their lives that he wants them to discard. Invite them to imagine these things as objects on a table in the Temple courtyard.

Say: 'Imagine a person behind that table offering them to you. Imagine Jesus turning the table over (turn the table over, if you have one). Imagine Jesus chasing the person out: out of the courtyard and out of your life. Imagine Jesus returning, smiling at you and welcoming you into his kingdom. Now you can have that relationship with God as it should be.'

Walking with Jesus

A meditation on our response to Jesus

This meditation could be used after hearing about Peter denying that he knew Jesus (for example, Luke 22:54-62) or after a reading of John 21:15-19. To prepare, encourage everyone to sit comfortably and feel relaxed. You might play some soft music in the background and allow for a short period of silence before beginning.

Imagine yourself walking into the dining room of a house. There is not much furniture, but in the centre of the room are a table and chairs. The table is set as if for a meal. There is a large basket of warm, fresh bread and an open bottle of wine. There is no one else in the room, but you feel at home and are happy to be there. You sit down at the table. What can you see? What can you smell?

As you are sitting at the table, the door opens and Jesus walks in. He is pleased to see you. How do you feel to see him?

Jesus sits beside you at the table. He offers you some bread and a cup of wine. As you are eating, Jesus asks you a question. Using your first name, he says, 'Will you follow me?' What is your response?

When you have finished eating, Jesus invites you to walk with him. You go out of the house and into a beautiful garden.

The sun is shining, it is a lovely day. As you are walking, Jesus turns to you. He looks sad. He asks you another question. Again he uses your first name, saying, 'Have there been times when you didn't want to know me?'

You tell Jesus the truth about those times. He listens patiently, without criticising or commenting.

As you walk on through the garden, you come to a gate which leads out onto the street. Jesus stops, and speaks to you again. He tells you that he knows about all the times when you have turned away from him. His words are gentle, and you feel a sense of relief in hearing them. What do you want to say to Jesus now?

When you have finished talking, Jesus explains that he has to go. He opens the gate to leave, and as he goes he turns to say goodbye. He tells you that you can come to this place to talk to him any time. Then he closes the gate behind him and walks away. How do you feel?

When you reach the end, allow a short time of silence. Then explain quietly that the reflection has ended, but encourage people to sit silently or pray for as long as they choose.

He couldn't love me!

A meditation on Peter's denial of Jesus

All of us have the same basic needs. Obviously there are the physical needs of food, drink and sleep but there are also emotional needs, such as wanting to be accepted and loved, and wanting a purpose so that we feel that our lives are not totally meaningless.

The physical needs are pretty easy to deal with but the emotional ones seem to be a lot harder because so often we don't feel accepted. Sometimes it's because of ourselves: perhaps we have done something that we feel ashamed of or we have failed in something and feel inadequate. Other times we're affected by those around us or perhaps by what we see on TV or hear on the radio: we're told that we're not good enough or we don't look right – too fat, too short, too spotty, whatever. Perhaps we're rejected by those we look to for love.

So we go around carrying this burden of guilt, shame, inadequacy or failure. And we try to hide it but it gets in our way. And it gets bigger and bigger. And we go into situations expecting to be rejected even before others have had a chance. 'They wouldn't be interested in me. They won't like me.' Perhaps we might even start behaving in a way to ensure that we get the reaction that we expect – a self-fulfilling prophecy, as they call it.

And we expect the same treatment from God. 'He couldn't love me, he couldn't accept me. I'm not good enough.' Well, that isn't the case. Before Jesus was crucified, Peter totally disowned him three times. 'I don't know the guy,' he said. And yet Jesus invited him back into friendship.

Jesus offers the same opportunity to each one of us. He can give us a sense of being loved and accepted, of having a purpose in life. Do you want that?

Stories for children

For children aged 8+

Holy week story with props
The story from Palm Sunday to Judas' betrayal

You will need: a sheet of green paper, a bag or pillowcase, rope, a coat, a paper palm leaf, a cardboard crown, a large stone, a water jug, a place setting, bread, a cup, a bag of coins

Before the session, attach numbers to each of the props: 1 rope, 2 coat, 3 paper palm leaf, 4 cardboard crown, 5 large stone, 6 water jug, 7 place setting, 8 bread, 9 cup, 10 bag of coins. Place them in a bag or pillowcase. Make a palm leaf by folding a sheet of green paper in half lengthways and then tearing around the edges to make an oval leaf shape. Tear a few slits to make fronds.

To begin the story, bring the rope out of the bag and point out the number 1. Explain that it is the first clue in the story. Tell the story as follows, bringing out the relevant props at each stage.

1 rope: Jesus and his disciples were at the Mount of Olives. He sent two disciples ahead to the next village to look for a young donkey that was tied up. It had never been ridden. The owners were astonished to see some men untying their donkey, but the disciples explained, 'The Master needs it', just as Jesus had told them to.

2 coat: As Jesus rode towards the city, a crowd gathered and threw their cloaks on the ground to show their love for Jesus and to make a soft path for the donkey.

3 palm leaf: Others in the crowd broke off palm branches and waved them to welcome Jesus.

4 crown: The people shouted, 'God bless King Jesus' and 'Glory to God'. Many called Jesus 'King' and wanted him to become their new ruler.

5 stone: The Pharisees were annoyed because they wanted all the honour and respect for themselves. 'Command your followers to be quiet!' they shouted, but Jesus said, 'If they keep quiet, the stones in the street will start shouting!'

6 water jug: Some days later Jesus sent Peter and John off to get the Passover meal ready. 'As you go into the city,' said Jesus, 'a man carrying a water jar will meet you.'

7 place setting: Peter and John found the man who led them to an upstairs room. They prepared the food and laid the table. Later all the disciples gathered to celebrate Passover together.

8 bread: At the end of the meal, Jesus gave them some clues about what was going to happen. He took some bread, said a prayer of thanks and broke it into pieces. 'Eat this and remember that my body will be broken for you.' The disciples weren't at all sure what Jesus meant.

9 cup: Then he shared a cup of wine with them all. 'Take a sip and remember that my blood will be poured out for you. I want you to share bread and wine in this way again,' said Jesus. 'It will be a special way of remembering me.'

10 coins: Jesus looked around the table; he knew that one of the disciples had accepted thirty silver coins in exchange for promising to betray him. Judas slipped quietly away.

If your group already knows the story well, give them the props and the two Bible passages (Luke 19:28–40; 22:7–23), and challenge the children to decide how the props fit the story and in what order.

It is finished!
An eye-witness account of the resurrection

Read the script below as if you are reliving what happened. Read it as expressively as possible, pausing where indicated.

'It is finished.' Those were his last words – 'It (Pause.) is (Pause.) finished.' The disciples thought it was finished. It was the end of Jesus as far as they were concerned. They'd seen him die and they had buried him, hurriedly wrapping his body in cloths and watching as the soldiers pushed a big, heavy stone across the entrance of the tomb. What a mess! What a crazy way for it all to end! A horrible, painful death on a cross and a rushed burial in a borrowed tomb before everyone packed up to rest on the Sabbath day. (Pause.)

It's now sunrise on the day after the Sabbath. Three women are going to the tomb to embalm Jesus' body. That means they'll put sweet-smelling spices on it. They didn't have time to do it when they buried him.

Let's listen to what they are saying as they walk along. They sound worried, and they are asking each other who is going to move the stone so they can go inside the tomb. But the guards aren't there – they've gone! Who's going to help them move the stone now? Wait! *(Pause.)* The stone's been moved already! Have the guards taken Jesus' body away?

They rush inside to check if Jesus' body really has gone. *(Pause.)* It has.

But… the tomb isn't empty – there's a man in dazzling white there! He's saying, 'Don't be afraid!' Don't be *afraid*? Of course we're afraid! What's going on? Where's Jesus' body?

But what's he saying now? Jesus has risen from the dead. No! Impossible! Or… maybe not, for Jesus…

What's that about telling Peter and the others? It's too much to take in! This is scary!

Jesus can't have come back to life! *(Pause.)* Or *can* he?

At the garden tomb

A story activity which interprets the resurrection story with tableaux

In advance, use a large sheet of paper to make a paper circle approximately 50 cm in diameter.

To prepare, help everyone find Mark 16:1-8 in their Bibles and read the verses out. Then invite the children in groups of three or four to look at the Bible verses they have just read and choose a point in the story to represent. Explain that they have five minutes to come up with a tableau portraying that point in the story. (A tableau is like a still photograph with the children 'frozen' in position.) Remind them to look at the story carefully, as there are actually several distinct parts to it: the women setting off for the tomb; the women, on their way, discussing what to do about the stone; the women arriving at the tomb.

When the five minutes are up, ask each group to share their tableau with the others. Challenge the other groups to guess which part of the story is being shown.

If you have a camera available, take photos and then display. (You must have parental permission to photograph the children.) If you have a large group you may wish to allocate the groups different parts of the story and break it down as

follows:

- The women preparing to go to the tomb.
- Their discussions on the way about moving the huge stone.
- Their arrival at the tomb and finding the stone already moved.
- Meeting the man in white robes.
- The women's hurried and fearful departure.

If you have a small group, you may wish to repeat the exercise to cover the whole story.

Hands-on Bible story

A resurrection appearance based on Luke 24:36-49

To prepare, ask the children to draw round their two hands. They should cut out one hand as drawn. On the other they should cut off three paper fingers, leaving the index finger and thumb, so that they have the shape of a hand pointing to something. Make one spare hand to represent Jesus with a nail wound marked in the middle. Clear away the scissors and waste paper. Discuss how the paper hands are not real hands – they are simply the same shape, created by drawing round the real thing. Ask everyone to look at their real hand. What is it made of? (Flesh, bone and so on.)

The children should each choose one of the disciples and write the name onto their hand with five fingers. The eleven disciples present were Peter, Andrew, James, John, Philip, Bartholomew, Thomas, Matthew, James, Simon and Judas (not Judas Iscariot). As the group sits around a table (or in a circle on the floor), get the children to place their whole paper hands on the table or floor in front of them and to hold on to the pointing hand. Read the following story.

The disciples were all together in the same room sharing a meal together. (*Indicate that the disciples are represented by the paper hands on the table or floor.*)

Suddenly Jesus appeared in the room. (*Put the 'Jesus' hand in the centre.*) He hadn't been there before, and he didn't walk through the door, so the disciples were absolutely terrified! They shook with fear. (*The children shake their pointing hand.*) They pointed at Jesus with their mouths hanging open with amazement. (*They point to 'Jesus' with the pointing hand.*) Jesus pointed to each of them in turn.

'Why are you all frightened?' he asked. 'Don't you remember me telling you that after three days I would come back to life? I know all this is a bit scary for you, but come and see for yourselves who I am. It's me – Jesus! I'm not a ghost. I have a body with real flesh and bones and I can prove it. Look at my hands and feet, and come and touch me.' No one spoke. There was a stunned silence of joy and amazement.

Finally Jesus said, 'I'm hungry! Can I join you for dinner?' So they made space for him to join them at the table and gave him a plate of fish. (*Rearrange the disciples' hands enough to make space for 'Jesus' to join the circle.*) Everyone watched Jesus as he ate his food.

'Ghosts don't eat food,' they said to each other as they pointed with wonder at his empty plate. (*Point to Jesus' place at the table or on the floor.*) Jesus explained the situation. 'You ought to know from reading the Bible that I had to suffer, but then I would rise again three days later. That is exactly what happened. Now you can tell the world about how everyone can be forgiven. Stay here in Jerusalem for now. You will need some help if you're going to tell my story to the world. I'll send you the Holy Spirit to come and help you to do just that. After that, it's up to you to tell the world!'

So the disciples waited for the Spirit to come and then they started on the job of telling the world about Jesus. (*Point the hands away from the disciples' hands and 'out into the world'.*)

Spot the mistake
Thomas' experience of seeing the risen Jesus

Divide the children into groups and give each group a sheet of paper, a pen and a Bible. Read aloud John 20:19–31 and invite them to follow in their Bibles. Then, ask the children to listen as you read the story below. It contains ten mistakes. Pause when you make a mistake (shown in bold). Challenge the children to discuss the mistakes quietly within their groups, decide on the correct word(s) and write their answer down each time.

The disciples were afraid of the Jewish leaders, and on the evening of that same Sunday they locked themselves in a **car** (*room*). Suddenly, Jesus appeared in the middle of the group. He greeted them and showed them his **feet** (*hands*) and his side. When the disciples saw the Lord,

they became very **sad** (*happy*).

After Jesus had greeted them again, he said, 'I am sending you, just as the Father has sent me.' Then he breathed on them and said, 'Receive the Holy Spirit. If you forgive anyone's sins, they will be forgiven. But if you don't forgive their sins, they will not be forgiven.'

Although Thomas the **Triplet** (*Twin*) was one of the twelve **football players** (*disciples*), he wasn't with the others when Jesus appeared to them. So they told him, 'We have seen the Lord!'

But Thomas said, 'First, I must see the nail scars in his hands and touch them with my finger. I must put my hand where the spear went into his side. I won't believe unless I do this!'

Five years (*A week*) later the disciples were together again. This time, **Timothy** (*Thomas*) was with them. Jesus came in while the doors were still locked and stood in the middle of the group. He greeted his disciples and said to Thomas, 'Put your finger here and look at my **eyebrows** (*hands*)! Put your hand into my side. Stop doubting and have **fish and chips** (*faith*)!'

Thomas replied, 'You are my Lord and my God!'

Jesus said, 'Thomas, do you have faith because you have seen me? The people who have faith in me without seeing me are the ones who are really blessed!'

Jesus worked many other miracles for his disciples, and **all** (*not all*) of them are written in this book. But these are written so that you will put your faith in Jesus as the Messiah and the Son of God. If you have faith in him, you will have true life.

Encourage the children to shout out the answers as you read this version again, and to give themselves one point for each correct answer (shown in brackets).

Jesus begins his journey

The story of Jesus' entry into Jerusalem told using clay

You will need: a copy of the diagrams on page 28, some modelling clay or clay tiles, cutters, rolling pins

Chat with the children about what they might expect a king to wear and ride when he entered an important city. Explain that Jesus wore simple clothes and rode a young donkey. He wasn't the sort of king people were expecting. Give each child some modelling clay and modelling tools, and give them some time to experiment. Challenge them to make models to illustrate the story as you tell it. If you have children in your group who find modelling difficult, prepare some clay tiles for them to etch with a sharp pencil.

Read Mark 11:1–11 from the CEV or GNB. Pause in the following places to allow the children to make their models. Use the suggestions below and the diagrams provided to help the children see how they could do this. (If you use the GNB, make sure the children understand that a colt is the young of a donkey.)

Read verse 1. Help the children to make the Mount of Olives. *(Suggestion: Start with a large and a smaller ball of clay. Roll one end of the balls with your hands to create pointed mountain peaks. Place the two peaks next to each other.)*

Read verses 2 and 3. Help the children to make the young donkey. *(Use your hands to roll a cylinder for the body and five smaller cylinders for the legs and tail. Make a ball for the head. Use your fingers to gently squeeze two ear shapes from the top of the head. Join your pieces together.)*

Explain that one of God's prophets long ago had said that God's king would ride on a donkey. The people thought that Jesus was the king God had promised.

Read verses 4–9. Help the children to make cloaks and leaves. *(Use a rolling pin to roll out some clay. Cut out some cloak and leaf shapes with a sharp pencil or clay cutter.)*

Read verses 9 and 10. Ask the children why they think the people were shouting words of praise to Jesus. (Entertain all their answers.) Explain

that some people thought Jesus was going to help the Jews defeat the Romans who lived in their country, so this made them very excited.

Read verse 11. Help the children to make houses to represent Jerusalem. *(Make several balls of different sizes with your hands. Squash the balls to make cube and cuboid shapes. Arrange your buildings together and add windows and doors with a sharp pencil or clay cutter.)*

Story with expressions

The story of the Last Supper

You will need: a copy for each child of the picture on page 29 or enlarge the picture and display it where everyone can see it clearly

Explain that every year the Jews had a special meal, called Passover, to remember the time when God helped their great, great, great … grandparents escape from slavery in Egypt. Jesus and his friends had gathered in a room in Jerusalem for this special meal, but the friends didn't realise just how special it was going to be. Jesus had something very important to tell them.

Ask the children to find someone in the picture who is looking sad and to copy that expression on their own faces. Then say:

While Jesus was eating he said, 'One of you who has been eating with me will tell my enemies where to find me. I am going to die, just as the Bible says.'

Ask the children to find a face in the picture that shows how they think the disciples would have felt on hearing Jesus' words. Challenge them to copy that expression. Say: One of the friends, Judas, said, 'You surely can't mean me!'

'One of you who is eating with me will betray me!' Jesus replied. (And later, it was Judas who betrayed Jesus and told his enemies where to find him.)

Later, during the meal, Jesus took some bread. He blessed the bread and broke it. Then he gave it to his friends and said, 'Take this and eat it. This is my body.'

Ask the children to find someone looking puzzled in the picture and to mimic that expression. Say: The friends did not understand what Jesus meant. They were even more puzzled when he

Stories

picked up a cup of wine and said that it was his blood. He said that when he died God would make it possible for people to be forgiven for the wrong things they did.

Finally, ask the children to find someone looking surprised, and to mimic that expression. Say:
After the meal, Jesus told his friends that that very night they would all run away. Peter was surprised and said, 'Even if all the others pretend they don't know you, I never will!'

Jesus replied, 'I promise you that before a rooster crows tonight, you'll say three times that you don't know me.'

But Peter said, 'Even if I have to die with you, I'll never say I don't know you.' And all the others said the same thing.

Ask the children to think about the story they've just heard and to make a facial expression showing how it makes them feel. Are they: sad, puzzled, frightened, surprised? Give each child the opportunity to say why they are making that expression.

Explain that Jesus told his friends all these things so that they would know what was going to happen to him. Ask the children if they know what would happen next. Encourage them to stay very quiet for a minute and tell Jesus how they feel.

Jesus prays
The story of Jesus' arrest

You will need: an area with comfortable seating, music (suggestions as follows):

Sad music:
Barber Adagio for strings
Barber Violin Concerto 2nd Movement
Beethoven Moonlight Sonata
Beethoven 'Pathetique' Symphony
Bruch Violin Concerto 2nd Movement
Elgar Cello Concerto 1st Movement
Elgar 'Nimrod' from *Enigma Variations*
John Williams Theme music from *Schindler's List*

Noisy music:
Mussorgsky 'Baba Yaga' from *Pictures at an Exhibition*
Richard Strauss 'Battle Scene' from *Ein Heldenleben* Op 40
Holst 'Mars, the Bringer of War' from *The*

Planets
Wagner *The Ride of the Valkyries*

Prepare a room or corner of a room and make it darker (but not completely dark). Play some sad music quietly. Also have some louder, violent music ready for later in the story.

Lead the children into the darkened area. Play sad background music quietly. Invite them to sit while you tell them the following story. (If you don't have the darkened space, encourage them to sit very quietly and close their eyes while they listen.)

One night, Jesus went with his friends to a place called Gethsemane. When they got there, he asked them to sit in the quiet garden and pray. Then he took Peter, James and John a little way away, and he said to them, 'I am so sad that I feel as if I'm dying. Stay here and keep awake with me.' Then he walked on a bit further and knelt down to pray to his Father God. 'My Father, if it is possible, don't make me suffer this. But do what you want, and not what I want.'

Jesus got up and went back to Peter and the others and found them sleeping! 'Can't any of you stay awake with me for just one hour?' he said to Peter. Jesus needed the comfort of his friends because he was afraid. He knew that he was going to die, because this was the only way everyone could be forgiven for doing wrong, but that was so frightening.

He went away to pray again and said, 'My Father, if there is no other way, and I must suffer, I will still do what you want.'

Jesus came back and found his friends sleeping again. They couldn't keep their eyes open. So he went to pray the same prayer again.

This time when Jesus came back he woke his friends up saying, 'Are you still sleeping and resting? The time has come. Get up! Let's go! My enemies are here!'

Change to the louder music and invite the children to stand up with you.

As Jesus said this, his friend Judas came into the garden. He'd brought a large mob with him who had swords and clubs in their hands! (Judas had told them that they should arrest the man he greeted with a kiss.) Judas walked right up to Jesus and said, 'Hello, teacher.' Then Judas kissed him. The men grabbed Jesus and arrested him. One of Jesus' followers pulled out a sword and cut off the ear of a man in the crowd.

Stop the music.

'Put your sword away,' said Jesus. 'Anyone who lives by fighting will die by fighting! Don't you know that if I wanted, God's angels would come to protect me? But that is not God's plan. I am choosing to let this happen.'

Explain that Jesus chose to be arrested and to die so that we can be forgiven for all the wrong things we do. Ask: 'What would you like to say to Jesus about that?' Give a short time for the children to make their response.

Hammer and nails
The story of how Jesus died

You will need: one short plank of wood and one long plank of wood, hammer, nails, cardboard, some clothes, some straws or matchsticks, a sponge

Tell the children you want to make a wooden cross. Position the short plank of wood about a third of the way down the long plank. Hold it steady and invite the children to take turns hammering the nails into the wood. Ensure that each child has a turn and that it's safe! Explain how to do it carefully!

Lay the cross on the floor and sit around it. Explain that you are now going to read from the Bible and that the children need to imagine they are Jesus' friends watching this happen.

Read John 19:16–19. Write the words 'Jesus of Nazareth, King of the Jews' on the cardboard, or ask a confident writer to do so. Put the sign at the top of the cross.

Read John 19:20–22. Tell the children that some people were not happy with what was written on the sign. They still didn't believe that Jesus was their king. Did Pilate change the sign?

Read John 19:23,24, showing the clothes and the straws or matchsticks.

Read John 19:25–30, showing the sponge. Ask the children what the soldiers gave Jesus to drink. What did Jesus say after he drank?

Ask the children how this story makes them feel. Do they know where Jesus was going? If not, read John 13:3. Tell the children that Jesus' death was part of God's big plan to make things right with his people. Explain briefly that this includes us. It is because Jesus died that we can be forgiven and be friends with God. Invite the children to say prayers of thanks to Jesus for dying so we could be friends with God.

Some children may wish to take this further. You may find the leaflet *Me and Jesus* (Scripture Union, ISBN 978 1 84427142 9) useful in helping them understand the gospel more fully. It's written in language appropriate for 5- to 8-year-olds, and is available from www.scriptureunion.org.uk/shop.

Story in a parcel
The Easter story with a game

Make up a parcel as for 'Pass the Parcel' with the following items, starting from the centre: party items (for example, party poppers, blowers, streamers, hats), a cardboard question mark, a white cloth, a large pebble, a picture of a dark night (or a sheet of black paper), a packet or jar of spices, a woman's headscarf (or use pictures from page 30). Provide suitable, quiet music and set up your sound system.

With the children, explain that after his last supper with his friends Jesus was arrested and nailed to a cross. When Jesus was dead a rich man called Joseph asked for his body and put it in a tomb, a cave cut in the rock that he had prepared for himself when he died. He had a huge stone rolled in front of the tomb so that no one would be able to disturb the body.

Say that although the story seems very sad so far, today is actually a special celebration so you are going to play a party game. Sit the children in a circle, put on some music and ask them to pass the parcel round the circle. When the music stops, allow the child holding it to unwrap a layer of the parcel and find an item. Allow the children to suggest what each item might represent, then comment as follows:

Headscarf – Ask who would wear one of these. (A woman.) Explain that the first people to find out that Jesus had come alive again were three women: Mary Magdalene, another Mary, who was the mother of one of Jesus' disciples, and a lady called Salome.

Stories for children

Spices – Read Mark 16:1. Explain that in the time of Jesus it was the custom to put sweet-smelling spices on a body when it was dead.

Night picture – Read verse 2. Ask the children why they think the women went out so early. (To go as soon as the Sabbath was over.)

Pebble – Ask why the stone might be a problem. Read verse 3. Ask how they would be able to get into the tomb. Read verse 4.

White cloth – Ask the children what they think the women were expecting to see in the tomb. Read verses 5 and 6.

Question mark – Ask how they think the women felt when they heard what the young man told them. Read verses 7 and 8. Explain that it was an amazing thing to be told. No wonder the women were frightened and confused.

Party poppers – Explain that the women did go and tell the disciples the good news. A few days later they met Jesus and saw that he really was alive. Ask the children how they think the women felt then.

My best friend Jesus
The story of Thomas with pictures

You will need: two large sheets of card, one with a simple cross drawn on it and the other with a picture of the risen Jesus showing his hands with the nail marks (see pictures on page 31)

Display the picture of the cross, hiding the other card underneath. Gather the children in front of the picture with their own space around them. Tell them that they are going to imagine that they are Thomas, one of Jesus' friends. You are going to read out Thomas' thoughts. They will be able to listen quietly and have time to think and talk to God. Use the script below, pausing briefly where indicated.

Jesus was my best friend. He was everyone's best friend. It's hard to believe he is dead. But I know he is. I saw the soldiers nail him to that cross. Later I saw that rich man, Joseph, take his body away. Jesus was wrapped up in white cloths and put in a cave. He was definitely dead. It happened on Friday. *(Pause.)*

And now it's Sunday. I've just called in to visit my other friends. I thought they'd all be as sad I am. But I can't believe it. They are all happy. They are saying they've seen Jesus alive again. They are saying he was here. How could he be here? I know he is dead. I saw it all on Friday. *(Pause.)*

But my friends keep saying Jesus is alive. Well, I don't believe it. And I won't believe it unless I see him for myself. In fact, I want to see those nail marks in his hands and I want to touch them before I'll believe. That's the only thing that will convince me. *(Pause.)*

Suggest that the children think about how Thomas is feeling as they walk about the room. Tell them to imagine a whole week is going by. Then ask them to sit down again.

It's Sunday again. I've had a horrible week. I've been miserable about Jesus being dead and my friends still keep going on about him being alive. I can't understand...
(Turn the card over to show the picture of the risen Jesus.)
He's here! It's Jesus! He's saying, 'Here are my hands, Thomas. Come and touch me.' But I don't need to. I just say, 'My Lord and my God.' *(Pause.)*

Jesus is still talking to me: 'Thomas, do you believe I'm alive because you've seen me? There will be many other people who will believe in me even though they can't see me. *(Turn the card round to show a blank side.)* They will be truly blessed.'

I think I understand what Jesus means. I knew all about him. I had seen the wonderful things he could do. I had seen the difference in my friends after they had discovered Jesus is alive. I think I should have believed.

One day some of my friends may write about Jesus. It will be the most important part of God's big story. People will discover Jesus is alive even if they haven't seen him for themselves. Perhaps you are one of those people. Think about my story and decide whether you believe in Jesus.

(Pause. Allow time for the children to think silently about this.)

Mount of Olives

Start with a large and a smaller ball of clay.

Roll one end of the balls with your hands to create pointed mountain peaks. Place the two peaks next to each other.

A young donkey

Use your hands to roll a cylinder for the body and five smaller cylinders for the legs and tail. Make a ball for the head.

Use your fingers to gently squeeze two ear shapes from the top of the head.

Join your pieces together.

Cloaks and leaves

Use a rolling pin to roll out some clay. Cut out some cloak and leaf shapes with a sharp pencil or clay cutter.

Jerusalem

Make several balls of different sizes with your hands. Squash the balls to make cube and cuboid shapes. Arrange your buildings together and add windows and doors with a sharp pencil or clay cutter.

Story with expressions

Activity on page 24

Activity on page 26

Stories

30

My best friend Jesus

Activity on page 27

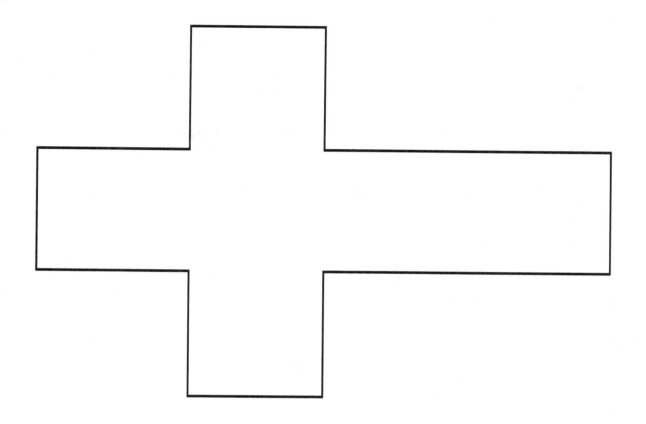

Jesus rides a donkey
The Palm Sunday story with movement

As you tell this story, invite the children (and any adults) to come with you to join the crowd following Jesus.

It's morning. The sun shines brightly as Jesus and his friends walk along the road. They are going towards a big city, called Jerusalem.

Sometimes they sing as they walk along. Now other people come and join them. Children skip along with their mums and dads. They are all going towards the big city. Let's go with them...

Jesus is quiet as he walks along. He's going to the big city too. He calls to two of his friends. 'Go ahead,' he says, 'you'll find a young donkey that has never given anyone a ride before. Please bring him to me.'

Jesus stops and waits. All the people stop too. Let's stop with them... What is going to happen? Listen! They whisper to each other, 'Is Jesus going to show us that he's our king?'

Listen! What's that sound? It's the clip-clop clip-clop of donkey's hooves on the road. Here come Jesus' two friends and they've brought the donkey with them. They lead the donkey to Jesus. They take off their coats and put them on the donkey's back. They help Jesus get on. Off they go again, with Jesus riding on the donkey. Come on, let's go...

Now what's happening? Look! The people in the crowd are taking off their coats too! They are laying them down on the dusty road, all the way along the road to the big city. Listen! They are shouting, 'Jesus is our king! He's coming to our big city. Now everything will be good for us again.'

Jesus tells the donkey to walk on. The people in the crowd cheer and wave. They watch as Jesus rides the donkey along the road and over the people's coats! Everyone cheers again! 'Hurray for Jesus! Hurray! Here comes our king, riding on a donkey!'

All the way into the big city the people cheer and wave. Let's shout and wave too...

Jesus is still quiet. He looks ahead, towards the big city. It's a happy day but Jesus knows that soon he will have to do something very hard; something that God wants him to do.

We'll hear more about that another time, but just for now, let's follow the crowd and shout with them: Jesus is our king! Hurray for Jesus!

A special meal
An account of the Last Supper

You will need: props such as a dressing gown, cloak or headdress, tables and chairs (all optional)

Pretend that you are one of Jesus' friends. You could put on a costume to show that you are pretending to be a different person. Sit with the children and tell the story in character.

I'm one of Jesus' best friends. We've had lots of meals together, but tonight we are going to have a very special meal – it is called a Passover meal. This is a meal when we remember how God saved our families hundreds of years ago.

I asked Jesus where he wanted to have the special meal. He said, 'When you see a man carrying a water jar, follow him to the room where we'll eat.' Jesus had got it all planned out. Can you help me get the room ready? (Organise tables and chairs. Pretend to put out plates and cups.)

After the meal, Jesus said something that was strange. 'This is the last meal I shall eat with you before I die,' he said. Well, we were all amazed! Was he really going to die so soon?

Then he broke up some bread and gave us each a bit. 'I want you to remember me always,' he said. 'When you eat bread, remember me.' (Pretend to give out some bread.)

Then he took the cup of wine and gave us each a drink. 'When you drink this wine, remember me,' he said. 'Remember my death as well as my life.' (Pretend to pass round a drink.)

(You can stop here or carry on with the story.) 'You are all my friends,' said Jesus. 'But one of you is going to hand me over to some soldiers to die.' We were really shocked to hear that. (All shake your heads and say, 'Not me!') 'I won't let you down!' declared Peter, one of Jesus' friends. 'You can trust me!'

Stories for children

'Oh Peter,' said Jesus sadly. 'You will say three times that you don't know me, before the cock crows.'

We couldn't believe it! It all felt very sad and mysterious. The only good thing was that Jesus seemed to be in charge. It was as if he knew exactly what would happen and it was all planned out. Somehow this meal and Jesus' dying must all be part of God's plan.

Come out of character and ask the children what they think will happen next. Reassure them that it will all work out right in the end.

In the garden with Jesus

Jesus' prayer in Gethsemane and his arrest

If you wish, use props such as a dressing gown, cloak or headdress.

Pretend that you are one of Jesus' friends. You could put on a costume to show that you are pretending to be a different person. Tell the story in character.

I'm one of Jesus' friends. We've just had a special meal with Jesus. He said he was going to die soon and that we must remember him. Now he's gone off to a garden. Let's go with him. *(Move off with the children round the room.)* Look! There he is, praying in the garden. Can you hear what he is saying to God? He's saying, 'Please, Father God, help me.'

I don't know about you, but it has got so late and I feel really sleepy. *(Yawn. Lie down and pretend to go to sleep. The children may or may not copy you. Suddenly, pretend to wake up.)* Oh look! Here's Jesus back again. Oh, I should not go to sleep, while he is praying.

He's going off to pray to God again. He's praying, 'Please, Father God, help me. Help me to do what you want.' I want to pray about doing what God wants too, but I feel really tired. I'll just lie down for a moment. *(Lie down again and pretend to sleep.)* Oh look! Jesus is back again. I think God must have answered his prayer.

(You may want to stop the story at this point or carry on in character.) Now some soldiers are coming! Do you think we should fight them? Get your swords ready! *(Pretend to draw your swords.)*

Oh! Jesus is telling us to put our swords away. *(Pretend to do this.)* 'This isn't a time for fighting,' says Jesus. 'I am ready to go with these soldiers.' The soldiers are taking Jesus away to die. I'm scared! What if they want to take me too? I think I'd better hide! *(Run off and crouch down as if hiding. The children may or may not copy you.)*

Come out of character and take off your costume. It all seems to be going wrong for Jesus. His friends have left him and he has been taken away by soldiers. But God has a plan. He is going to help Jesus and his friends. Can anyone guess what will happen? *Reassure the children that everything turns out right in the end.*

What Mary saw

The resurrection story told with a puppet

Beforehand, make a simple puppet to represent Mary, one of the women who followed Jesus. Draw a face on a wooden spoon and drape a piece of fabric around it. Otherwise use a doll dressed in a long piece of cloth.

Tell the children that today's Bible story is about Jesus. Tell the story through the puppet as follows:

Hello! My name is Mary. I've been one of Jesus' friends for a long time. I love him so much. That's why I and his other friends were so sad and afraid when bad things began to happen to him.

Soldiers took him away and we didn't know what was happening. Then we heard that he was going to die. The soldiers took him to a hill near the city. They put him on a cross.

It was Friday. We went to the hill. We wanted to be near him, although we didn't understand why someone as good and loving as Jesus should be killed like that.

We were there when he died. Before he died he said, 'Father God, please forgive the people who are doing this to me.' It was just like Jesus to be so kind even to those who were hurting him. The sky turned dark as though it was night-time.

When they took his body down from the cross, we watched and followed them to a garden, where they put Jesus into a tomb made from the rock. We saw a huge stone being rolled in front of the cave.

We were so sad. We thought we would never see Jesus again. So we went home and stayed there until Sunday morning. Then I said, 'We should go to the garden and look after Jesus' body. We can take spices and perfumes.'

So, just as the sun was rising, we set out. When we got to the garden, I said, 'Look, the stone has been rolled away from the tomb.' We ran to see what had happened and we saw two angels there! They said, 'Jesus isn't here. He's alive again. Go and tell Peter and his other friends.'

How surprised and amazed we were! But, do you know, the angels were right? We saw Jesus with our own eyes. He was alive again!

Jesus is real

Thomas sees and believes

Tell the following story, using exaggerated facial expressions (happy, amazed and so on) and changing the pace and pitch of your voice to create excitement, puzzlement and surprise.

Mary knew that Jesus had come back to life. She had seen him. She told everyone else the wonderful news. Mary was very, very happy.

Some of Jesus' other friends had seen Jesus too. One evening, Jesus' special friends were sitting together in a room. As they were talking, Jesus appeared! The friends were amazed. How had Jesus come through a locked door? Could it really be Jesus? Or was he a ghost?

Thomas, another friend of Jesus, wasn't in the room with the others. So, when they saw him again, everyone said excitedly, 'Guess what, Thomas? We've seen Jesus. He's alive. Isn't it wonderful?'

But Thomas wasn't happy and excited. 'I don't believe you,' he said. 'I haven't seen Jesus.'

Later on, as the friends were sitting talking, Jesus appeared again. This time, Thomas could see the person looked like Jesus. He touched Jesus' hands and his side. He knew then that Jesus was a real person.

Thomas was so happy. 'Jesus!' he said. 'Now I know you really are alive!'

Review why Thomas knew Jesus was real: he saw him, he spoke to him, he touched him – he knew it was Jesus!

Can you tell the children, in a very few words, how you know Jesus is real?

Easter craft

Egg painting
Decorating eggs in keeping with the Easter story, for older children

You will need: a copy of the picture on page 38, a blown or hard-boiled egg for each child, paints, table covering, cover-up and clean-up equipment

Before the session starts, check that your paints work on the eggs.

Look at the picture of Jesus breaking bread on page 38. Ask the group whether this is the kind of picture they had in mind as they think about the Easter story? If not, how is it different?

Challenge everyone to paint a picture (or two) onto an egg, choosing any scene they want from the Easter story.

Make arrangements for everyone to carry their eggs home without breaking them, or keep them in church to be a part of a 'Resurrection Exhibition'.

Something to wave
A 'make' for Palm Sunday for children

You will need: a copy of instructions on page 39 for each child, sheets of A4 paper (white and different colours), small sticks such as garden canes or lengths of dowelling rod (alternatively, use drinking straws or pencils).

Give each child a copy of page 39 which shows them how to make something to wave just as the crowds waved palm branches to welcome Jesus into Jerusalem.

Divide the children into pairs or threes to make a flag, a banner, or a streamer stick. They can either make one each or work on one together. Allow up to ten minutes and offer help if necessary.

When the flags, banners or streamers are finished, invite each small group to show the others what they have made. Use them to praise King Jesus!

Bad news into good
A paper-cutting exercise with a message, for older children

You will need: copies of the instructions on page 40

Give out copies of the instructions, pairs of scissors and a plain sheet of A4 paper. Help everyone to cut and fold the paper as shown in the diagrams. Show them how to arrange the pieces to form a cross, and then the word 'Alive'. Suggest that they take their pieces of paper home and show their families how the resurrection turned bad news into good news.

Paper craft
Paper weaving with an Easter message, for older children

You will need: a copy of page 41 for every person (printed on thin card, if possible), a ready-made example

Show everyone your example. Cut out the two strips, and cut the slits on piece A. Make sure nobody cuts beyond the marked lines. (You might want to cut the slits beforehand with a craft knife.) Weave strip B in and out of A – see the instructions on page 41. Pull tab C so that the words change.

An Easter tree
An Easter decoration for older children to make

You will need: two or three branches, white paint, a vase, eggs, a long needle, materials to decorate the eggs, ribbon

In some countries people make an Easter tree decorated with eggs for the middle of their table. They put it out about a week before Easter. This idea is suitable for older children, young people and adults to make. Younger children would need plenty of help.

Choose two or three leafy branches or find some bare branches and paint them white. Arrange the branches in a vase.

Decorate some eggs to hang on your tree. To do this, blow the centre from each egg so that they don't go rotten. Make a hole in both the top and the bottom with a long, strong needle. Gradually enlarge the hole at the bottom. Push the needle through the hole and swirl it around to break up the yolk. This will make it easier to blow the egg out of its shell. Cup your mouth around the smaller hole and gently blow the egg out into a basin. (You could use it for scrambled egg or baking cakes!) Blowing the egg out takes patience and a lot of puff.

Rinse the empty shell with warm water and leave to dry. Carefully decorate the egg shell with felt-tip pens, stickers, ribbons, sequins, food dye, spray paint, glitter and any other materials you have. Thread a length of ribbon onto a long needle and pass it through the small hole in the top of the eggshell, starting from the larger hole at the bottom.

Tie a knot at the bottom and a loop in the top so that it can be hung on a branch. You can also add yellow ribbons, mini chicks and other Easter decorations to your tree.

Easter cube

A card cube which tells the Easter story

You will need: page 42 copied onto card for each child, glue sticks, mini Easter eggs (optional)

Help the children to make the Easter story cubes. Glue the sides together. Get the children to leave one flap open if you have mini Easter eggs to put inside the cubes. The completed cubes can be used to retell the Easter story.

Seed crosses

A simple craft to encourage people to think about God's plan

You will need: sunflower seeds

Read out loud Jesus' words from John 12:24. Explain that Jesus was talking about himself when he said that a seed (or grain of wheat) would die and then bring new life. Let everyone glue the sunflower seeds onto sheets of paper in the shape of a cross, as a reminder that Jesus died as part of God's plan, so that we could be forgiven and have new life.

Make a bookmark

An easy craft with a prayer response

You will need: a piece of A6 sized paper for each child

Follow the instructions on page 43 to make the cross bookmarks. A larger one could be made with A4 paper as a demonstration.
Ask for suggestions as to what they could draw or write on their bookmarks. Some people may want to say thank you to Jesus for dying on the cross for them. Others may want to say sorry for the wrong things they have done, and ask for forgiveness. Allow time to finish the bookmarks.

Suggest everyone takes the bookmarks home to keep in their Bible or another favourite book where they will see it often.

Posters

You will need: dull and bright paint in trays, pieces of paper, including two which are poster-sized, hand-washing facilities

Let everyone make dull and bright handprints on separate papers. As the paint is drying, talk together about how each part of the Easter story is important. Palm Sunday reminds us that Jesus is our King. The second part of the story reminds us that he was willing to die for us.

Cut out the best handprints. Glue the bright ones on one large background and the dull ones on another. (They could be arranged to make a crown and a cross shape respectively.)

Provide pens for everyone to write words praising King Jesus between the bright handprints, and words thanking him for dying for us amongst the dull ones.

Easter garden

Individual models of the Easter garden to take home

You will need: copies of the template on page 44, paper fasteners, glitter, streamers

Before the session, photocopy the model template onto thin card – one for each child. Give the copies out and invite the children to colour the tomb and stone.

Help them to cut out the parts of the model, fasten the stone to the tomb with a paper fastener and attach the stand. Together roll back the stone and read what the angel said. Glue streamers and glitter on the inside picture and let it dry before closing!

Paper tearing

A simple way for children to make a cross from paper

Easter craft

You will need: instructions and diagrams from page 45

Using the instructions and diagrams, take the children step by step through folding and tearing a sheet of paper. Give them plenty of time to copy what you are doing and help them as necessary. They will love the surprise when they open out the sheet of paper!

Easter egg-people
A fun activity for younger children

You will need: card ovals (egg shapes) in different colours, wiggly eyes, stickers, wool, chenille wires, glue, glitter

Talk about how we give each other chocolate eggs at Easter time and that makes us happy; but there is an even better reason to be happy. The best news about Easter is that Jesus is alive.

Let each of the children choose an egg shape and decorate it to make happy Easter egg-people. Give them wiggly eyes and a smiley mouth, and use fun things to give them hair (glitter, chenille wires, wool, and so on).

Make an Easter storybook
An easy activity for younger children

You will need: the pictures on page 46 for each child, scissors, glue, collage materials or crayons, paper

Fold an A4 piece of paper in half for each child and help them paste one picture on each page. The pictures can be coloured in or decorated with collage materials. Talk to the children as they work about what each picture means and encourage them to use the books to tell the Easter story in their own words.

Easter scene
A messy activity with a dramatic result, suitable for younger children

You will need: materials to make an Easter scene from paper and collage materials, a large sheet of blue paper (painted blue and allowed to dry if necessary); black paper cut into a cross, a large hill, a large stone, the sun (see page 47 for shapes to copy); paints in trays with scrunched-up kitchen paper for printing, cover-up and clean-up equipment; or brightly coloured stickers

or pens suitable for work on black paper

This activity turns a dark picture into a brightly coloured one. Show the children the black shapes and place them on the blue paper, to illustrate the sad part of the Easter story.

Remind them that God turned the sad day into a good day. Say that we can make the picture show this by putting bright colours on one side of the black paper.

Take the shapes off the background and let the children paint them, with different groups or individuals working on each piece. If necessary, allow time for the pieces to dry.

Lay the pieces out again, black side up, on the blue background. Say, 'Jesus died on a cross. The sky grew dark and all his friends were sad.'

Then as you say, 'But God turned the sad day into a good one,' turn all the pieces over. Add, 'Jesus was alive again!'

Easter cards
A fold-up card for younger children

You will need: copies of the template for an Easter card on page 48, art materials

Demonstrate folding one copy of the template twice, to make a card with the cross on the front. Each small picture on the card tells part of the Easter story.

Let the children colour and decorate their own copies. It is easier if they do this before folding. Help them to fold the paper so that it stands up as a greetings card.

Easter banner
A messy activity with a message for display

You will need: a large sheet of paper, thick wax crayons, thick black paint, washing-up detergent, blunt knives or wooden spatulas

Get everyone to help cover a large sheet of paper with thick wax crayon in lots of colours. Paint over it with black paint that contains a squeeze of washing-up detergent. When it is perfectly dry, scrape away the words 'Happy Easter!' to reveal the colours underneath. Display the completed poster in church for the congregation and visitors to enjoy.

Craft

JESUS BREAKS BREAD

Something to wave

Activity on page 35

Paper

Card

Hooray
for
the King!

Sticky tape

3 cheers
for Jesus!

Sticky tape

Dowelling, pencil
or drinking straw

Jesus is
the best!

Two sheets of A4 paper stuck
together with sticky tape

Sticky tape

Twin strips of
coloured A4 paper

Wrap the paper around a
pencil to make it curl

You will need a plain sheet of A4 paper and some scissors.

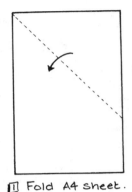

① Fold A4 sheet.

② Fold

③ Fold

④ Cut into thirds.

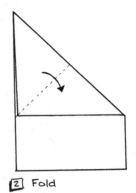

⑤

Arrange the pieces to represent Jesus' death on the cross.

1 The cross
2 Two nails
3 The sign above the cross
4 The two criminals who died beside Jesus
5 The stick with a sponge soaked in wine
6 Two sad friends watching

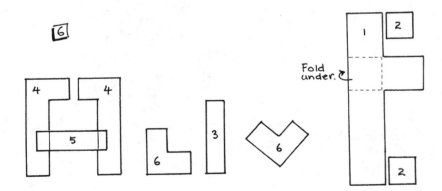

⑥

Fold under.

Rearrange the pieces to spell out what happened to Jesus three days after he was killed – the bad news became the good news of Easter! Check out Mark 15 and 16 for the whole story.

Craft

Paper craft

Activity on page 35

Slider B

But God showed how much he loved us by having Christ die for us, even though we were sinful. But there is more! Now that God has accepted us because Christ sacrificed his life's blood, we will also be kept safe from God's anger. Even when we were God's enemies, he made peace with us, because his Son died for us. Yet something even greater than friendship is ours. Now that we are at peace with God, we will be saved by his Son's life. Romans 5:8-10 (CEV)

OW GO CH

Card A

Instructions

How to make your own NUCI!
NUCI = now you see it

1 Cut out card A and slider B. Carefully cut along the eight dotted lines in the middle of card A – don't cut right to the edge! Colour them in if you want to.

2 Weave the slider in and out of the card, so that the words, 'Own Goal Chaos? appear.

3 Pull Tab C on the slider gently to change 'Own Goal Chaos?' into 'Now – God's child!'

4 Now you see it!

Craft

41

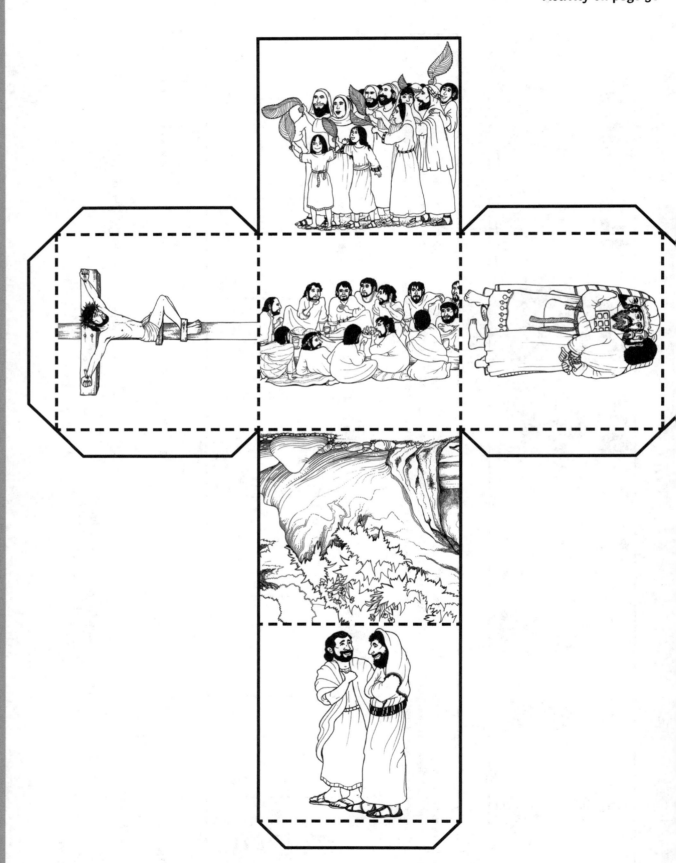

Make a bookmark

Activity on page 36

1

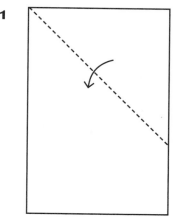

Fold diagonally to match other side

2

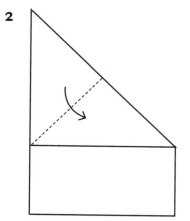

Fold diagonally again to match side

3

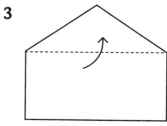

Fold bottom panel up

4

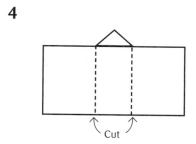

Cut off side sections

5

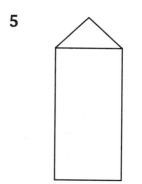

6

Unfold to reveal a cross

Craft

43

Craft

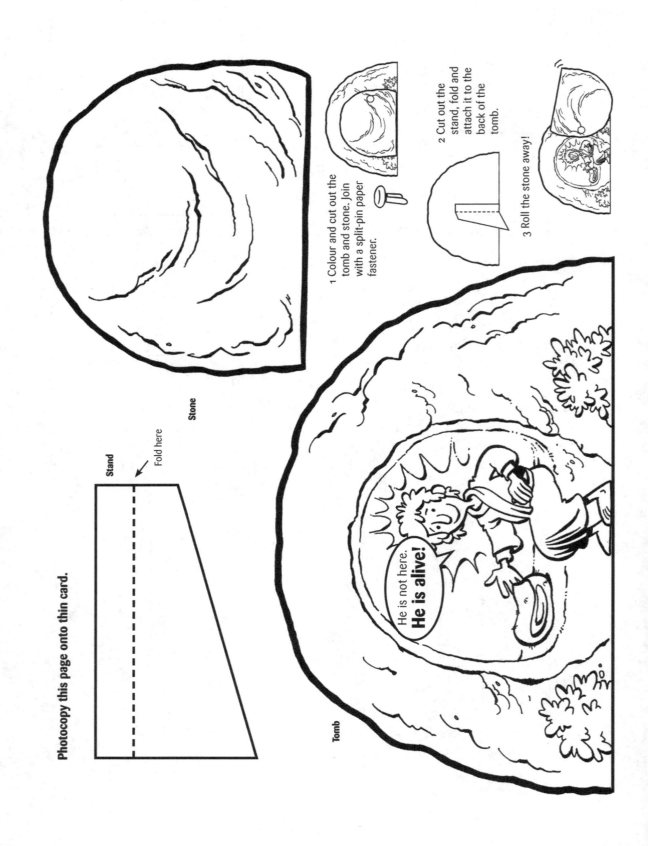

Stone

Stand

Fold here

Photocopy this page onto thin card.

Tomb

He is not here.
He is alive!

1 Colour and cut out the tomb and stone. Join with a split-pin paper fastener.

2 Cut out the stand, fold and attach it to the back of the tomb.

3 Roll the stone away!

Paper tearing

Activity on page 36

 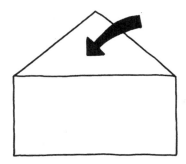 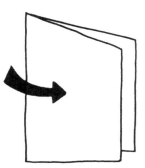

1 Fold the top left-hand corner over to meet the right-hand edge of the paper.

2 Fold the top point of the triangle across to the bottom-left point.

3 Fold in half.

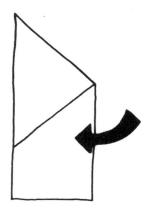

4 Fold in half lengthways.

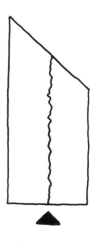

5 From the middle of the square end, tear in half.

6 Open out the largest piece to see the cross!

Activity on page 37

Craft

46

Easter scene

Activity on page 37

Activity on page 37

Craft

All-age services for Palm Sunday

The King's decision
Ideas for an all-age service on Palm Sunday

Bible passage: Luke 19:28-40; 22:39-48

Aim: To worship Jesus as our King and Saviour

Introduction
Begin the service with a traditional Palm Sunday hymn or song or other items which bring worship to Jesus, our King. Intersperse the items which follow with other suitable hymns or songs.

Following orders
With: long strips of paper for each volunteer and instructions for folding a palm cross on page 54

Ask for four volunteers from the congregation (mixed ages). You may wish to decide on these in advance. Tell them that they are going to be given a set of instructions, which they need to follow word for word and within a set time limit. Give them each three strips of paper and the instruction sheet. Point out that these instructions are complicated; this is not an easy task. (If you have a video camera and projector you can have close ups of the volunteers making their crosses projected on a screen.) When the time is up commend all of your volunteers for their efforts and the completed palm crosses that have been made.

Use the activity to introduce the theme of Palm Sunday, explaining if necessary that in many churches crosses made from palm leaves are given out at this time. They act as a reminder of the day Jesus rode into Jerusalem and many people waved palm branches to honour him as king.

Make the point that folding the crosses involved not giving up but following instructions through to the end. Similarly Jesus didn't give up; he followed through his Father's instructions - right to the end, even though it meant his death on a cross.

Prayer ideas
With: the words of Luke 19:38 and Zechariah 9:9 displayed on a screen, or large pieces of card, sheets of paper with the words 'King' and 'Saviour' written out

The aim of this time is to worship Jesus as our King and Saviour. Display the two Bible verses, Luke 19:38 and Zechariah 9:9. Read aloud the verses and say that they remind us that Jesus is both our King and Saviour.

Get everyone to form small groups of three or four people, and give a piece of paper and a pen to each small group. Ask everyone to note down suitable words to describe Jesus, or things to be thankful for about him, beginning with each letter of the words 'King' or 'Saviour'. The two verses will give some words to start off with, for example, King, gentle, Saviour, righteous (NIV), and then they should add others.

After a few minutes invite volunteers to call out suggestions for each letter which should be collated and projected on a screen or flip chart. Try to select at least one word beginning with each letter. The leader should either use these ideas and weave them into a prayer of thanks to Jesus, or suggest that within their groups everyone is encouraged to praise Jesus, using some of the words from their own group list, or the combined list.

Parade
With: several prepared actors, chosen music, extra coats and jackets, old sheets, paper 'palm branches'

Explain that you will invite everyone to join in a dramatic re-enactment of the events of Palm Sunday. Tell everyone that they are to play the part of the crowd in Jerusalem, so they should be ready to wave their hands or coats in the air, cheer loudly or rattle a bunch of keys as the procession enters. Distribute the old sheets and palm branches for children to lay on the floor for the actor playing Jesus to walk on. Play some music and invite everyone to wave and cheer as the actors enter and walk down the aisle of the church. When the procession reaches the front, turn down the music and stop the cheering.

Remind the congregation that we can offer our own worship to Jesus here and now. Invite everyone to join in a worship song such as 'Hosanna, Hosanna', or 'You are the king of glory'.

Bible-reading mime
With: one prepared volunteer to read the Bible passage and four actors to mime

This activity could follow on immediately from the parade (see above). The contrast between the noise of the parade and the solitude of Jesus on the Mount of Olives is very important.

Read out Luke 22:39-46, pausing at the appropriate points below whilst other volunteers mime as follows:
Verse 39: 'Jesus' walks onto stage and two 'disciples' follow.
Verse 40: Jesus walks away from group and kneels.
Verse 43: As Jesus is praying, another volunteer comes forward and puts their arm around him.
Verse 45: Jesus walks back to the group – the volunteers playing the disciples are now slumped against each other or some furniture (for example, a pillar) as if asleep.
Verse 46: The disciples wake up looking a bit embarrassed as Jesus approaches.

All the actors then quietly leave the stage.

All-age talk
With: a pair of socks plus several 'odd' ones, a football scarf or team shirt, 'variety pack' of breakfast cereals (optional)

We are faced with choices every day of our life. From when we get up – What shall I have for breakfast? Does it matter what socks I wear today? – or when we go to bed – If I stay up to watch the football on TV will I be tired in the morning? *(Produce your props as you discuss each item.)*

In life we have lots of choices to make. Sometimes we know where these choices will lead. (Yes, to stay up late will make us tired in the morning, and sometimes it does matter if our socks don't match.) Sometimes we don't know the outcome of our choices.

Let's take Jesus and his friends. They had lots of choices to make in the stories we have heard today.

Disciples' choices
Jesus' friends had to decide whether to go and get the donkey as Jesus said, or to go and find a great stallion. That choice mattered – Jesus needed to ride into Jerusalem on a donkey. It showed he was the king who had been promised long ago (Zechariah 9:9), and it showed what kind of king he would be – humble and not proud or fierce.

His friends also chose to go with him to the Mount of Olives. That was a good choice – they were supporting a friend in a time of need. But

then they fell asleep while he prayed – a bad choice (see Luke 22:46)!

Jesus' choices
But it is Jesus' choices that are most important. Jesus knew that riding into Jerusalem where everyone could see him would make the Jewish leaders very angry. Jesus knew what was about to happen – that they would want to get rid of him by killing him. He asked God, his Father, to spare him, but then said he only wanted to do what God wanted. He wanted to follow his Father's instructions. Jesus also knew that to die on a cross was the way to take the punishment for everyone else. He died so that everyone who believes in him can be forgiven. Jesus chose to be both our King and our Saviour.

Our choices
Letting Jesus be our King and our Saviour involves making a choice too: do I want to follow Jesus and worship him?

Prayer
With: music of your choice

Allow time for the congregation to reflect on what Jesus had to suffer to be our King and Saviour. As you play some quiet music, encourage the congregation to consider the choices Jesus had to make as he went towards the cross.

As the music continues, ask, 'What might you like to say to Jesus because of what he has done for you?' Allow further time for individuals silently to express personal prayer, or encourage people to say their prayers aloud, if appropriate.

If you have younger children in the congregation provide paper and crayons for them to draw a picture of Jesus as their response.

Further worship
With: songs of choice and the words of the Bible verses below projected onto a screen or on handouts

We are all called to worship our Lord no matter what age we are. When some people tried to stop the children calling out praise to Jesus, his response was to quote from Psalm 8, verse 2: 'From the lips of children and infants you, Lord, have called forth your praise' (Matthew 21:16 NIV); so use songs and words from the Bible to praise Jesus together.

Leader: 'Blessed is the king who comes in the name of the Lord! Peace in heaven and glory in the highest!' (Luke 19:38)

Sing together one of the following: 'You are the King of glory'; 'Lord I lift your name on high'.

All: 'Blessed is the king who comes in the name of the Lord! Peace in heaven and glory in the highest!' (Luke 19:38)

'You laid aside your majesty', 'Thank you for saving me', 'Thank you Jesus'.

Leader: 'A very large crowd spread their cloaks on the road, while others cut branches from the trees and spread them on the road. The crowds that went ahead of him and those that followed shouted, "Hosanna to the son of David!" "Blessed is he who comes in the name of the Lord!" "Hosanna in the highest heaven!"' (Matthew 21:8,9 NIV)

Sing one of the following: 'Ride on, ride on in majesty'; 'We want to see Jesus lifted high'.

Turning the tables

Ideas for an all-age service for Palm Sunday

Bible passage: Matthew 21:1-17

Aim: To welcome Jesus into our lives as Lord

Celebrating Jesus

With: face paints, coloured paper, balloons, plastic bottles, rice or lentils or other dry seeds, red ribbons, felt-tip pens, sticky tape, other craft materials

The events of Palm Sunday invite us to engage corporately in the sense of 'being one of the crowd', in ways that are familiar at, say, a football match, and yet not (usually) at church. To this end, begin the service with some activities that will help to create a carnival atmosphere. You could paint 'J's on the children's faces (ask permission from parents first). You could make and decorate paper hats with the name 'Jesus', or write it on balloons. Encourage everyone to use percussion instruments (home-made is OK!) in worship.

Give everyone in the congregation a ribbon to wear or wave around. If possible, use red or purple ribbon. Red is the traditional Palm Sunday colour, and purple usually denotes royalty (the

people of Jerusalem were welcoming him as king).

When everyone is equipped to 'welcome' Jesus, sing songs of worship together and encourage everyone to enter freely into a spirit of celebrating Jesus' presence with them.

Prayer idea

With: small candles or tea lights (if possible, use either red or purple candles to continue the theme of kingship and Palm Sunday), matches, tapers, a tray of sand

Place the tray of sand either on the floor or on a low table, making sure there is plenty of space around it. Ask an adult to stand near the table with matches and tapers, to help the children light their candles. Distribute candles to everyone. Explain that each person should spend a few moments thinking about something they want to say to Jesus. Then they should light their candle and place it in the sand, praying their prayer to Jesus as they do so. For example, they could: express thanks and joy for all that Jesus has done and continues to do in their lives; pray a prayer for someone they know who has no faith; say 'Sorry' to God for something they have done.

All-age talk

With: the celebration 'props' made for the earlier 'Celebrating Jesus' activity, a flip chart and marker pen

Pose this question to the congregation: 'If you had been in the crowd that first Palm Sunday, what would it have been like?' Invite responses from people of all ages and write them up on the flip chart. Hopefully the responses will show that the story of Palm Sunday is a story of contrasts: Jesus and his disciples have come to Jerusalem from the countryside, not from a throne room or a stately palace, and they have walked in on bare or sandalled feet. Jesus has deliberately chosen an undramatic entrance: he has ridden into a major city on a borrowed donkey, not in a royal chariot. Of course, we know now that all this is true to Jesus' character (he has resisted previous attempts from the people to make him 'king' according to their own ideas about a king). And yet at the time, these things turned the people's expectations on their heads. But they cheered him into Jerusalem all the same.

Pause at this point to invite the congregation to celebrate once more in praise of Jesus, using the 'props' they made at the start of the service. Encourage everyone to proclaim Jesus because they have heard him, met him or been healed by him.

After the 'crowd celebration', make the point that Jesus causes a reaction: his arrival threw the whole city into turmoil and celebration. People were asking 'Who is he?' and the crowd was responding to the question as best they could. Jesus welcomed their enthusiasm even if their faith or understanding was not complete. These days and in our culture, we don't do spontaneity easily. Therefore, we need to engage again with what Jesus has done for us, so that we can proclaim him to others, untroubled by how much, or how little, we understand of the mystery. We need to rediscover and express our enthusiasm for Jesus.

Conclude by referring to Jesus turning over the tables in the Temple. Ask the congregation for their reaction to hearing that Jesus behaved in this way. Does it turn their expectations about him on their head? Make the point that Jesus was angry because in turning it into a marketplace, the people had turned the purpose of the Temple upside down – it was no longer a place where people could go and pray to God. The Jesus we welcome is one who challenges us to live as God intended. That can mean turning our lives upside down in obedience to him. What, then, is our reaction to Jesus now?

Banners
With: large sheets of card or thick paper, felt-tip pens or paints

Ask the congregation to gather together in small, mixed-age groups. Give each group a large sheet of card or paper and some felt-tip pens or paints. Invite the children in each group to come up with a slogan about Jesus (such as 'We love Jesus!' or 'Jesus is King!'). For the children, the act of deciding on their own slogan can be a powerful statement of personal faith, in an environment (church) where often their faith is expressed second-hand through parents. Each group should then work together to create a banner bearing their chosen slogan. Ask the children in each group to bring their banner to the front and display it to everyone.

Sing a celebratory song together, ending with everyone waving their materials and making lots of noise!

Sound and vision
Play a video clip of crowds celebrating together. Footage from a large sporting event or from a music concert would be appropriate. Alternatively, find an audio clip of a large crowd and play that at various points during the service.

Imaginative meditation
This activity provides the congregation with an opportunity to explore and reflect creatively upon a contemporary equivalent to Palm Sunday.

Ask everyone to imagine a celebratory crowd scene that they would like to be part of. One person might want to imagine going to the world première of their favourite movie. If anyone has been to a première like this, invite them to share their experience. Others may wish to think of being at the football or rugby World Cup final, or on the victory parade when a national team returns after a great victory. Perhaps the imagined scene could be the day of the Queen's coronation, or the experience of being backstage at a concert by a favourite band.

Ask everyone to close their eyes and picture their chosen scene in their minds. Now lead them in an imaginative meditation to enable them to enter into that scene for themselves. Use a meditative, descriptive style rather than factual or linear storytelling. For example: 'Relax your shoulders. Close your eyes if you feel comfortable. Put yourself at the scene of ... What is the first thing you see? What sounds can you hear around you? What emotions are you feeling? Imagine this ... Listen to that ... Look around you ... the person you've been waiting for has arrived. Walk through the crowd and try and get as close as you can to them.'

After a while, and with everyone keeping their eyes closed, explain that many of the feelings people felt as they imagined their particular scene were present in the crowd that watched Jesus ride into Jerusalem on a donkey. Invite everyone now to imagine that scene. How might they have felt to see the King of kings so close up? Does he exceed, or indeed, even meet their expectations? Is he someone they have wanted to meet for ever? Someone they have just heard about yesterday and are intrigued by? Or someone they are indifferent towards? Allow a few moments of silent reflection for members of the congregation to consider their response.

All-age services for Palm Sunday

Palm cross placement
With: palm crosses

Distribute palm crosses to everyone in the congregation. Explain that they are made from the leaves of palm trees, reminding us of the palm branches used by the crowd to welcome Jesus into Jerusalem on the first Palm Sunday. Bound into the shape of a cross, they remind us of the extent to which Jesus turned expectations upside down – dying on a cross so that people could receive forgiveness and welcome God into their lives.

Given the significance of these apparently simple palm crosses, ask everyone to think about where they might strategically place their cross around their home, workplace, car, or any other place of daily activity, so that it prompts curiosity and questions from their friends, colleagues and acquaintances in the week ahead. Invite everyone to say a silent prayer to God, committing to place their cross in the place they have thought of and to respond honestly and boldly to the questions it raises from those who see it.

Conclude by leading the congregation in a prayer expressing excitement at the prospect of being able to welcome new faces into the church in the coming weeks, as a result of conversations had by people of all ages in response to the display of their palm crosses.

Procession
Lead the congregation out in a procession with the banners made earlier in the service. You could process once round the building. Alternatively you could go even further afield, moving out into the local area and walking together as a congregation in an act of witness to those who live near to your meeting place. Children and young people would need to be properly supervised on any such procession.

1. Cut off three strips from the long side of a sheet of A4 paper. Each strip should be approximately 15 mm wide. One strip will be used to form the crosspiece. Join together the other two strips with sticky tape and use this longer strip to form the upright of the cross.

2. Make two folds on one end of each strip approximately 15 mm apart (Fig. 1 folds 1 and 2, Fig. 2 folds 3 and 4).

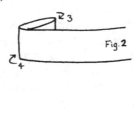

Fig. 1

Fig. 2

3. Join the two strips together by using the folds already made as a kind of 'hook' on the end of each strip (Fig. 3 folds 5, 6 and 7). You will now have a firm join at this crossover point. Make sure that the loose end of the crosspiece is to the right and the loose end of the longer strip hangs down over the front of the crossover point.

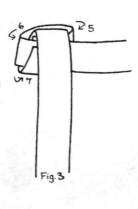

Fig. 3

4. Take the loose end of the crosspiece and fold it forward leaving a loop of paper of about 5 cm sticking out to one side (Fig. 4 fold 8). Pass the loose end underneath the long strip hanging down at the front.

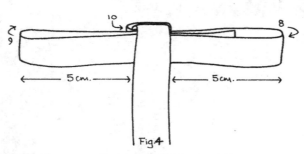

5 cm.   5 cm.

Fig 4

5. Form another loop sticking out 5 cm on the other side by folding the loose end of the crosspiece and tucking it into the back of the crossover point (Fig. 4 folds 9 and 10). The crosspiece should now stick out evenly about 5 cm either side of the crossover point.

6. The long strip should still be hanging forward over the crossover point. Take the loose end and tuck it upward through the loop at the back of the crossover point, pull the strip right through and a firm knot is formed (Fig. 5 tuck 11).

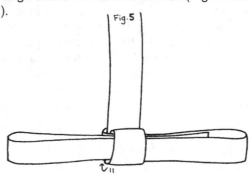

Fig. 5

7. Fold the loose end backward leaving a loop of paper sticking up about 7 cm to form the top piece of the cross (Fig. 6 fold 12). Take the loose end and tuck it down the back loop of the crossover point pulling it through until the top loop forms neatly (Fig 6 tuck 13).

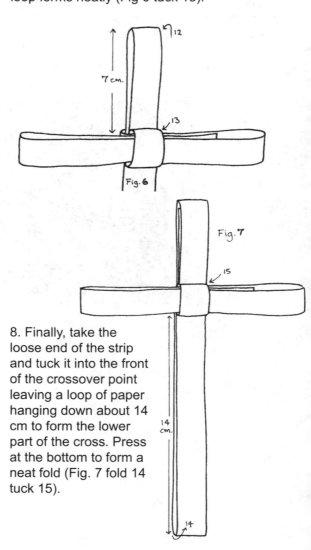

7 cm.

Fig. 6

Fig. 7

8. Finally, take the loose end of the strip and tuck it into the front of the crossover point leaving a loop of paper hanging down about 14 cm to form the lower part of the cross. Press at the bottom to form a neat fold (Fig. 7 fold 14 tuck 15).

14 cm.

On trial

Ideas for inclusion in an all-age service for Good Friday or in the preceding week

Bible passage: Matthew 26:57-68

Aim: To give thanks that Jesus was willing to be punished in our place

Game

With: questions which require the answer 'Yes' or 'No'; a stopwatch or kitchen timer plus 'time's up' signal (for example, whistle or cymbal), timekeeper, small prizes (for example, sweets)

Invite three volunteers of different ages to take part in the game. Explain that you will ask them each a number of simple questions, which they must answer truthfully, but without using the words 'Yes' or 'No'. If they can last for one minute without making a mistake they will be awarded a small prize.

Play the game by beginning to ask questions fairly slowly then building the pressure on the participant by adding in asides to trip them up, such as, 'Was that a yes, then?' At the end thank all of the participants and award a prize to the most successful.

Ask your volunteers how it felt to play the game. Admit that you were deliberately trying to trip them up so that they would give the answer you wanted. It was only a game and if they made a mistake it did not matter too much, but sometimes it does matter if we give the wrong answer.

Go on to say that in this session you will be thinking about the time when enemies of Jesus tried to trick him into saying things that would get him into a lot of trouble. They were not just playing a game – they were trying to find a way of getting rid of Jesus. But Jesus was ready to take the punishment even though he had done nothing wrong.

All-age talk

With: three paper chains, an actor to represent Jesus

If you played the 'Yes – No' game, refer to it and remind everyone that when someone is deliberately trying to catch us out we find it hard to stop ourselves from saying the wrong thing. When Jesus was arrested by the Jewish leaders they tried to find something they could punish him for, but he had not done anything wrong so they tried to trick him into saying something wrong instead.

Lies

(If you wish, project the word 'Lies'. Invite the actor representing Jesus to come forward and stand in a prominent place at the front of the room with his back to the congregation.)

After Jesus was arrested, the chief priests and leaders of the Jews called in some people to tell lies about Jesus. They said that they had heard him promise to destroy the Temple where the people came to worship God (Matthew 26:59,60). *(As you speak, slowly wrap a paper chain around him giving him the loose ends to hold, so that he is discreetly keeping the paper chain in place.)*

Jesus heard their lies and he knew he had not done anything wrong but he said nothing to defend himself (Matthew 26:62,63). The false witnesses could not agree on their own made-up stories. *(The first heading 'dissolves' from screen. The actor allows the paper chain to fall to the floor.)*

Trick questions

(Project the words 'Trick questions' and as you speak repeat the action with the second paper chain.)

Jesus' enemies asked him two 'trick questions'. They thought that he would still get himself into trouble whether he answered 'Yes' or 'No'. The chief priest asked Jesus, 'Are you the Son of God?' (26:63). Pilate, the Roman Governor, asked Jesus, 'Are you the King of the Jews?' (27:11–13). If Jesus answered 'No', they hoped that everyone would stop believing in him. If he answered 'Yes', they would accuse him of pretending to be equal with God (blasphemy) and of trying to take the place of the Roman Governor (treason).

Jesus was not caught out by the questions. He knew what they would say, but he spoke the truth and did not try to get out of it. They were all amazed at his answers. They knew that he was innocent but they did not want to believe in him (Matthew 26:64,65; 27:11). *(The second heading 'dissolves'. Allow the second paper chain to fall to the floor.)*

Mocking

(*Project the word 'Mocking'. As you speak, repeat the action with the third paper chain.*)

Although Jesus was completely innocent, the Roman soldiers led him away to be punished. They mocked him and beat him to make him suffer (Matthew 26:67; 27:29,30) but Jesus did not show anger or try to retaliate. (*The third heading dissolves.*)

Conclude by saying that Jesus' enemies thought that when they sent him away to be killed they had beaten Jesus. But Jesus knew that he would take the punishment instead of everyone else, and then it would be possible for us to be forgiven. (*Allow the paper chain to fall to the floor. The actor quietly walks away after you have finished.*)

Prayer of response

Lead the congregation in a prayer in which individuals can take the opportunity to thank Jesus for dying in their place.

Lord Jesus, I am sorry that you were treated cruelly.

I am sorry that you were beaten and tortured.

I am sorry that you had to die in my place.

But, I am glad that you came back to life and will never die.

I am glad that you have made a way for my sins to be forgiven.

Thank you for dying in my place. Amen.

The tree

This presentation can form part of a traditional Good Friday service. It is best presented with two dancers who can choreograph a simple dance together. One could represent the tree, following the movements suggested and the other illustrating the reactions of joy, turning away, sorrow and so on. At the words 'Now turn your gaze to this tree', the dancers could change roles, the second dancing the part of the second tree. The music chosen to accompany the dance should be gentle and sustained.

Here is the story of a tree –
Planted new at creation's dawn.
Think of its growing, burgeoning, blossoming

As the dance of creation
Brought life to all
In the garden of God.

Think of the joy as the tree
Grew in stature,
Stretching its branches to the wakening sky.
Think of God's pleasure,
The leaves maturing,
The fruit now appearing,
Swelling and ripening,
Its purpose complete.

For this is the tree
Set in God's garden,
The tree that brings harmony,
Healing and peace.
This tree is the tree of life.

But look again, listen.
The tree is rejected!
Do you see how we turn away,
Taking instead another tree's fruit,
A tree that offers knowledge and power,
The power to know how to hurt and destroy,
To spoil and to grab,
To devastate and kill?

Do you see the grief of God's sorrow
As we turn from his gift
To what is forbidden,
As we turn from new life
To darkness and death?

Now turn your gaze to *this* tree.
Axed down, cut from its roots,
Its leaves stripped, its boughs hacked,
Laid on bare earth.
In death, undignified.
Fashioned roughly to a cross.

Dragged to a hill,
Its precious wood pierced with nails
And stained with blood.

Then left against a darkening sky,
Outstretched to emptiness.
A tree of death.

But this tree bore the Lord of Life.
The nails that pierced its wood
Pierced him.
The blood that stained the tree
Redeemed the world.
And through the death a new way, a living way was opened,
A way of return to the garden of God,

To the Tree of Life,
To the fruit, ever fresh, that brings
Wholeness,
To the leaves that bring
Healing.

Suggested Bible reading: 1 Peter 2:21-24 (The Message)

'This is the kind of life you've been invited into, the kind of life Christ lived. He suffered everything that came his way so you would know that it could be done, and also know how to do it, step by step.
He never did one thing wrong,
Not once said anything amiss.
They called him every name in the book and he said nothing back. He suffered in silence, content to let God set things right. He used his servant body to carry our sins to the Cross so we could be rid of sin, free to live the right way. His wounds became your healing.'

Prayer

As we begin our Good Friday walk of witness, let us focus our thoughts on Jesus' walk to his death.

Lord Jesus Christ, you carried the cross to lift us from death to new life.

You endured cruel suffering that we might know love and mercy.

You bore taunting and jeers that we might know blessing.

We thank you. We praise you. We worship you.

May we walk Christ's way and live his new life to the glory of God: Father, Son and Holy Spirit.

The journey to the cross

A presentation with movement and words

Prepare the 'stage' with pairs of shoes of all kinds spaced around the area with, if possible, a large cross at the centre. The shoes mentioned below should be among those displayed and the 'readers' should know where to find the shoes they will be holding later. To begin, music is played which should be sombre but not overpowering. The readers' voices must be heard clearly over the music. The readers take their time coming singly or in pairs to the front and begin to walk around as individuals as though considering which shoes to choose. They continue to do this, pausing often until their turn to read comes, but coordinating their movements so that not all are moving or standing at the same time. When it is their turn to read, they pick up their shoes and move towards the congregation to speak. After they have spoken, they should go and stand at the foot of the cross holding their shoes or return to their seats.

Reader 1 Narrator
(Music. The other readers begin to come forward and move around.) The journey is about to begin. We will travel together to the cross, following Jesus, remembering what he has done for us. How are you journeying? How am I journeying? How serious are we about the journey to the cross?

Reader 2 holding party shoes
I want to take the journey to the cross, but I am wondering... Am I wearing the right shoes for the journey? These party shoes are nice, smart and shiny. I wear them to all the special occasions I attend, but I can't walk far before my feet begin to ache. They tell me the journey to the cross can be hard and long. Though my shoes are fine for special occasions – like coming to church a couple of times a year when something fun is happening – perhaps they are not right for following Jesus. I wonder what you think...

Reader 3 holding trainers
I want to journey to the cross, but I need to think carefully about the shoes I will wear. Should I wear my trainers? Some people might think they are not smart enough for following the King of kings. And yet they would support my feet – especially if I needed to get running, or do extra training to get fitter and keep up with what God wanted me to do. They are not elegant shoes, but they would show that I'm taking this seriously. I wonder what you would say...

Reader 4 holding slippers
I am going to make the journey to the cross. I am wearing my cosy, comfortable slippers. I think they will be all right. I wear them to laze around home and when I put my feet up in front of the telly. They are not made for hard walking, so I'm hoping it will be an easy journey and that all will go well. I shouldn't like to have to change much and I don't see why I should. I'm happy to follow Jesus as long as the way isn't too tough. My comfortable slippers will do, I'm sure. I wonder

what you think...

Reader 5 holding wellington boots
I am going to follow Jesus to the cross and I'm putting on my wellies. The way may be hard ahead. There might be bogs and raging rivers. I might have to face dark places in which I won't be able to see where I'm treading. The going might be tough and I'll rely on the strength of my wellies to see me through. I'll be following Jesus, you see, and he didn't promise an easy way for his friends. Yes, I'll put on my wellies. I'm determined. I wonder what you'll do...

Reader 6 holding shoes with holes
I think I ought to take the journey to the cross, but I only have my old shoes with holes in them. I'm not out to impress, though perhaps I should have mended these shoes a long time ago. They are in bit of a state. In fact, they are not much use; they let rain in and give me no protection. If I cared about my feet I wouldn't wear them at all. Now I'm wondering if I've left it too late to follow Jesus on the road to the cross. Are these the right shoes to wear? I wonder what you'd do if you were me...

Reader 7 holding walking boots
I am going to take the journey Jesus took – the journey to the cross. I think I will have to wear my walking boots. They are strong and hard-wearing. Whether the journey takes me up steep hills or into the deepest valleys, they'll give me the protection I need. I don't know the way ahead. I only know that I want to follow Jesus whatever that means. I'll keep the cross in my sights – and get walking. I wonder if you'll come with me...

Reader 1
Lord Jesus Christ, as we consider your journey to the cross, we ask you to accompany us as we seek to travel with you. May we walk as you did with courage and determination. Help us to take each step as an act of faith in your saving love for us. Amen.

All-age services for Easter Sunday

Death defeated

Ideas for a service for Easter Sunday

Bible passage: Luke 24:1-12

Aim: To celebrate that Jesus overcame death

Game
With: several volunteers

Volunteers stand together in pairs and stare at one another with 'blank' faces. The first person to smile sits down. Those who are still standing up then turn to each other and the game is repeated. Hands can be waved, jokes can be told, comments (nice ones) can be said, but smiling is not allowed. Put a time limit on the game. Applaud those who are still not smiling and congratulate those sitting down on being naturally 'smiley' people.

Explain that we all have emotions which are given to us by God, and we show many of them on our faces! When we are happy or sad we often can't hide it. On Easter Day we are celebrating that after Jesus died God raised him to life again and that should really make us smile!

Prayer idea
Encourage everyone in the congregation to form pairs and look at one another's faces. This may cause some laughter, or slight embarrassment, particularly for newcomers so don't dwell on this too long. Use either the following words or your own as an opening prayer. People can point to their own faces as each feature is mentioned.

'Dear Lord, thank you for our faces – our eyes, our ears, our mouths, our noses. As we gather together in your presence, help us to see with our eyes the joy of Easter in each other's faces; to speak out with our mouths the story of Jesus being raised to life; to hear with our ears the story of Easter in a fresh way; and in the same way that we have noses right in the middle of our faces, to keep you in the centre of our celebrations this morning! Amen.'

Worship idea
With: items to build a simple model of the empty tomb (a table, a large box, a piece of brown/grey cloth, a circular piece of card for the stone rolled back from the grave, some white cloth), background music and appropriate songs

As music is played in the background, build a simple model of the empty tomb to use as a focus for reflection. Bring the items forward one at a time and place them on the table. Allow a pause for reflection between each item. The items can be brought from within the congregation by prepared members, or brought out by a leader at the front.

The large box is laid on its side with its opening towards the congregation. This is draped with the sheet to represent the cave in the hillside. The 'stone' is placed to one side of the box. The folded white cloth is placed inside.

With the model in place as a focus, sing a suitable song, such as: 'He is Lord' or 'From heaven you came'.

All-age talk
With: paper, pens, faces from page 63 enlarged and printed on A4 sheets – you may need more than one of each picture, pegs and string (to stretch across the room if you do not have sufficient people to help)

Invite volunteers to hold up the faces, or peg them to the line, for the congregation to see. Explain that they represent various emotions, for example, happiness, sadness, fright, anger, puzzlement, wonder and disbelief.

Read out Luke 24:1–12, then run through the story as follows using either these words or your own, inviting people to suggest which would be the appropriate face for each part of the story. Encourage interaction with the leader. As each face is selected, invite forward the volunteer holding it, or ask a helper to reorganise the display line, as appropriate.

The Bible passage is broken down as shown below:

Verse 1: As it was the Sabbath from the Friday evening (sunset) to sunset on the Saturday, not only would they not have been able to visit the tomb to 'do things properly', they would have had lots of time to think about what had happened. How would the women have felt on the way to the tomb?

Verses 2 to 4: How did they feel when they couldn't find the body?

Verses 4 and 5: How did they react when they saw and heard the angel?

Verses 6 to 8: How do you think they felt when they were told such strange news?

Verses 10 and 11: How do you think the women and disciples felt both giving and receiving the news? Was it easy to talk about?

Verse 12: How did Peter feel?

Make the link with our own emotions. God did not create us to have only happy feelings – part of who we are is to have a full range of emotions and to express laughter, tears, joy and sadness.

On the day of the resurrection the women were shocked, surprised, then full of joy and probably tears.

Peter couldn't believe it. He had lied about his relationship with Jesus and betrayed him. Was it really possible that Jesus had come back to life? He had to find out for himself.

The empty tomb challenges us where we are. For some it's easy to accept the risen Jesus, for others it is difficult. How do you feel right now?

Hand out sheets of paper and pens. Because Jesus has come back to life, we can live with God for ever. Encourage everyone to draw a face that shows how they feel about this victory of Jesus over death. Ask if anyone would like to say why they have drawn the face they have.

Prayer response
With: faces from page 63 enlarged and printed on A4 sheets, pegs and string (to stretch across the room like a washing line)

Display the emotion pictures (faces) at the front of the room. Invite the congregation to turn in their seats and talk in small groups about each other's prayer needs and those of the surrounding community. For example, do we know people who are sad – what can we pray for? Who do we know who we could tell the joyful news to that Jesus is alive? What things have happened to make us happy? They may pray together now or promise to pray later.

At the end of the time a suggested closing prayer could be as follows:

Lord, thank you for the empty tomb; your victory over death. Help us to understand how we feel about this wonderful news, and how to explain it to other people who may not understand. Amen.

Sing songs which celebrate God's victory over death, for example, 'To God be the Glory!', 'I am a new creation' or 'He has risen'.

Risen Saviour
Ideas for an all-age service for Easter Sunday

Bible passage: Matthew 28:1–10

Aim: To worship Jesus as our risen Lord

Prayer idea
With: copies of the Easter story cartoon strip on page 64, meditative music either from a recording or provided by your musicians

Give everyone a copy of the Easter story cartoon strip. Ask everyone to look carefully at each of the individual panels, and consider the different stages by which the story unfolds and the different reactions of the 'players' in the drama. Play some meditative music in the background. Encourage them to think about which part of the story most closely reflects their own thoughts and feelings about Easter, and to bring those thoughts and feelings quietly and prayerfully to God. Reassure everyone that they do not have to be totally 'comfortable' with the concept or the truth of the resurrection. It took the disciples a significant amount of time to come to a full grasp of what was happening – and they were there! It will help us to be honest with ourselves, and with God, about our own excitement or confusion.

Easter surprise
With: Handel's 'Hallelujah Chorus' (or other suitably triumphant music), appropriate audio equipment, flowers, ribbons or some other materials with which to create an unusual centrepiece in your meeting room (see below)

Before the session, install a large visual centrepiece in your place of worship, to help everyone to think about the wonder of the resurrection. For example, if there is a central cross in the church, adorn it with flowers or ribbons to express the move from crucifixion to resurrection. Many churches like to have special flower displays for Easter; perhaps the arrangement could be displayed in an unexpected place to draw attention to its beauty and its embodiment of new life.

The Easter story is all about different people's reactions to the surprising fact of Jesus' resurrection.

All-age services for Easter Sunday

Set the scene for today's service by giving people an unexpected experience of Easter. Play triumphant Easter music (Handel's 'Hallelujah Chorus', for example) outside the church, if possible, so that expectations are already altered before they reach the door. If you normally serve refreshments after the service, you could serve them beforehand to welcome people. There are many possibilities; but whatever you decide to do, the aim is to draw people into a different set of expectations about their worship and whet their appetites for an experience of the unexpected.

Step inside
With: copies of the Easter story cartoon strip on page 64, meditative music either from a recording or provided by your musicians

If you chose not to use 'Prayer idea', give everyone in the congregation a copy of the Easter story cartoon strip now. If you did use 'Prayer idea', this activity follows on naturally from it. Play some quiet, meditative music, and invite the congregation to focus on the cartoon strip. Lead a series of reflections on the story from the perspectives of different characters at different stages: How were the guards feeling, moments before the earthquake? How were the Marys feeling as they approached the tomb? How did the guards feel at the arrival of the angel? Note that the women were also afraid: what was going through the women's minds as they hurried away from the tomb? What would they have felt at the moment they first saw Jesus? How would each of the characters involved have understood God's involvement in the events that were unfolding around them? Take some time over this so that everyone has the opportunity of stepping inside the Easter story and of trying to experience it from the perspective of the characters involved.

Role play and discussion
With: Bibles, a flip chart and marker pen

Divide the congregation by gender. Encourage them to cluster into small, mixed-age groups. Give each group at least two Bibles. Ask everyone to turn to Matthew 27:62 – 28:10. Lead them through the story one stage at a time, asking them to discuss in their groups the separate experiences of the guards (males) and the women (females) in the story. At each stage, guide them to consider:

What each group of people were expecting to happen;

How they reacted when events went against their expectations.

Allow the groups a few minutes to discuss each stage of the story amongst themselves. Then invite feedback from both groups. Write up responses on the flip chart.

When you've gone right through the passage, draw attention to the list of responses written down on the flip chart. Point out that the event of Easter causes different people to react in different ways, depending on their expectations and the nature of their relationship with Jesus. Pause to give everyone the opportunity – either individually or in the same groups – to consider or discuss how they feel about the resurrection of Jesus. Reassure everyone that they do not have to discuss their feelings in groups, if they would rather not. It is better to allow people to be silent than for them to feel compelled to say things they don't really mean.

All-age talk
With: a simple Easter tomb (for example, made with stacked cardboard boxes and tape), copies of your own paraphrase of Matthew 27:63,64 as a script for the guards, a pair of cymbals or other percussion instrument

Before the session, construct a simple Easter tomb from cardboard boxes to one side at the front of your meeting place. Paraphrase Matthew 27:63,64 and make copies, or use a version from *The Message*.

Choose a volunteer to play Pilate, another to be an angel, and three or four to act as chief priests and Pharisees. Give the 'chief priests' and 'Pharisees' copies of your paraphrase of Matthew 27:63,64 as their script. Divide any other volunteers into two groups: guards and women. Sit them on either side at the front of the room. Position the angel out of sight and Pilate in the centre at the front. Ask for an adult volunteer to sound the cymbals when the angel appears and when the earthquake strikes.

Read Matthew 27:62. Signal for your 'chief priests' and 'Pharisees' to make their way over to 'Pilate' and give him their message. Read Matthew 27:65. Signal for your group of 'guards' to join the 'chief priests' and 'Pharisees'. Invite them to march together round the room and then to the tomb at the front. Read Matthew

27:66. Ask the guards to secure the tomb with the material provided (such as string). Say that the guards were probably expecting Jesus' disciples. Read Matthew 28:1. Invite two 'women' to come to the tomb. Ask the 'guards' how they feel when the women appear. Did they mock or laugh at them? Ask the women to return to their group.

Turn and ask the women how it has felt to sit around for the past few minutes doing nothing. Say that's how the women in the Easter story spent the Sabbath. They saw where Jesus' body was, and left. On Sunday morning, though, they returned to the tomb (signal to the group of women to come to the tomb). Read Matthew 28:2-4, signalling for the cymbals and the 'angel' as you do so. The guards should fall down as though dead, and stay there. For the moment, their story ends...

Ask the 'women' how they feel arriving at the tomb to find 'dead' guards. Signal to your 'angel' to break the seal on the tomb (cut the string) and open it. Read Matthew 28:5,6. Invite the women to go nearer and look inside the tomb. Ask them how they feel about seeing the empty tomb. Read Matthew 28:7,8. Say that having looked into the tomb – where they last saw Jesus' body – the women left fearful and joyful. Make the point that this is not the end of their story because they then encountered the risen Jesus. Read Matthew 28:9,10. Signal to the 'women' to return to where they were sitting.

Conclude by contrasting the reactions of the guards and the women. Make the point that though there is a single Easter story, people experience it very differently depending on their attitudes to and views about God. Invite everyone to reflect on how they have responded to what they have seen and heard, and with which characters in the story they most strongly identify.

Easter letters to God
With: paper, pens or pencils

Say that both the soldiers and the women in this session's story were left with something that they needed to tell. Explain that in both cases the message was probably muddled and incomplete, given the events that had taken place. Ask everyone to pause for a few moments to consider what, in the light of this service, they want to say – and to whom – about the resurrection of Jesus.

Suggest that many people may have thought about someone who doesn't know that Jesus is alive. Explain that you would like everyone to tell someone about the resurrection, but not perhaps the person they have been thinking of.

Give everyone a sheet of paper and a pen or pencil. Invite everyone to write a letter to God, telling him how they feel about Jesus' resurrection. Say that our sense of the need to tell others about it can cause us to pass on the news without ever really stopping to reflect on our own feelings about it. Encourage everyone to be honest with God in their letters – no matter how muddled and confused they are. Stress that the letters can be as short or as long as they need to be and that they will not be shown to anyone or read out in public. Adults should be ready to help children as necessary – though it may well be that children will do this activity more easily than adults! Those who cannot or do not want to write can draw their response.

When everyone has finished their letters, ask them to read them silently to God. Suggest that everyone keeps their letter in a safe place where they can refer to it and reflect on how God is helping them grasp the truth and significance of the resurrection.

Death defeated faces

All-age services

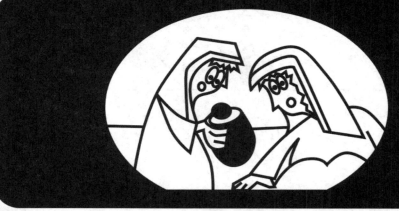

Creative prayer for Easter

Nineteen ideas to encourage people to respond to God creatively

Palm Sunday Praise

A prayer sequence for Palm Sunday for all ages together

You will need: five copies of Psalm 47:5–9 with a different verse highlighted on each

Beforehand, give the psalm verses to five people with loud voices or microphones, who are spread throughout the congregation.

Sing one or more songs that praise God as our King. Especially appropriate are those that echo the shouts of 'Hosanna!' on Jesus' arrival in Jerusalem, for example, 'Hosanna, hosanna'; 'You are the King of Glory'; 'Give me oil in my lamp', – using appropriate verses such as 'Give me joy in my heart, keep me praising' and 'Give me breath in my lungs, keep me shouting'.

Break into the singing at appropriate points, perhaps as background music continues to play, with those in the congregation holding the words from Psalm 47 reading out their highlighted verses in turn.

Palm Sunday shouts of praise

A praise activity for all ages together

You will need: written shouts of praise, each one on a separate piece of paper (for example, 'Hosanna! Hosanna!'; 'Jesus, our King!'; 'Thank you, Jesus!'

Point out that the Jerusalem crowd celebrated their coming king not knowing what sort of a king he was. We do know – he came to give everything, dying so we can be forgiven and have new life with God for ever. How much more reason we have to celebrate!

Ask the congregation to imagine that your centre aisle (or other equivalent area) is the route that Jesus is taking as he arrives in Jerusalem. The crowd laid in front of him whatever they had or could find. Ask the congregation what they would lay down if they were there now. Invite them to lay those things on the route – perhaps a coat or jumper (but encourage spontaneous responses).

Display or distribute the shouts of praise and invite people to call out some of these – or their own words of praise – with the whole congregation repeating each shout all together.

Shouting stones prayer

A prayer activity for Palm Sunday for anyone aged 7+

You will need: large stones (available from DIY stores or garden centres), fine-tipped permanent markers (make sure the children are given instructions about using them carefully)

Read or tell the story from Luke 19:28–40, reading or saying again Jesus' reply ('... if they keep quiet, the stones themselves will start shouting' Luke 19:40).

Give each person a large stone and a permanent marker pen. Challenge them to make their own 'shouting stone'. Get everyone to write a simple line of praise on the stone: for example, 'Jesus is king', 'Praise Jesus – he's worth it', 'Thank you Jesus for loving me'. They could decorate it with a mouth, a speech bubble or a palm branch.

Pray together and encourage people to each contribute the line they have written.

Hosanna prayers

A prayer activity for Palm Sunday for children aged 8+

You will need: paper palm branches (see page 70 for template) or scarves, a hat or box

Ask the children for suggestions of 'Easter' things they can thank God for (for example, 'sending Jesus'). Write each one on a separate strip of paper and place them in a hat or box at one end of the room.

Invite the children to make two lines (as if they are lining the streets), with palm branches or scarves to wave.

Invite one child to run up, collect a strip of paper from the hat and read it out (for example, 'Thank you, God, for... *sending Jesus*') as they walk back between the other children. Encourage everyone else to shout out words of praise while waving their branches or scarves. Repeat until everyone has had a turn.

Bread thanksgiving
A prayer activity for all ages

You will need: either cut-out paper 'loaves' and pens/pencils, or bread rolls on paper plates

Either: Distribute paper 'loaf' shapes to each person and give out pens. Invite everyone to choose one thing they are going to thank God for in response to hearing Luke 24:13–35 (the story of the walk to Emmaus), and then write or draw this on their paper loaf. These can be collected up and placed at the front of the church.

Alternatively: Pass around real bread rolls and as each person takes a small piece encourage them to give thanks, silently, to God for Jesus.

Washing feet prayer
A prayer activity for all ages

You will need: water-based paint, paper, washing-up bowls, washing facilities, newspaper or plastic sheet

Pour paint into the washing-up bowls and put down some newspaper or a plastic sheet to protect the floor. Remind people about the act of service Jesus used to symbolise his love for them – foot washing.

Invite those who wish to do so to remove their footwear and dip their feet in the paint and create a footprint on a sheet of paper. You could also do this by brushing the paint onto each foot to make a print, but the symbol of dipping each foot into a bowl can be helpful.

Clean up the 'painty' feet and clear the area. As you do so, read John 13:12–17 to the group. When the footprints are dry, encourage those who have taken part to decorate them with words describing how they can follow Jesus' example of serving others.

Close with prayer, thanking Jesus for his love to us, and for the strength so we can show that love to others.

Prayer wheel
Making a prayer aid for the six days leading up to Good Friday, for children aged 8+

You will need: a copy of page 71 for each child, split pins

Give each child a copy of the prayer wheel. Encourage the children to cut out and decorate their prayer wheels; perhaps play some worship music while they do this. Help anyone, where needed, to join the prayer wheel with the split pin.

Show the children how, on each day up until Good Friday, they can move the prayer wheel round to the next section and remember a different aspect of Easter. Encourage them to use the prayer wheel each day this week, and to use the ideas on each section to help them pray.

Make a twig cross
A prayer activity for all ages suitable for Good Friday

You will need: two pieces of wood or twigs and a piece of string 30 cm long per child, instructions on page 72

Remind everyone that many Christians use the cross as a symbol of Jesus' love for us – he loved us so much that he died for us. Explain that you are going to make crosses from twigs and string to remember this and to thank Jesus for his love.

Give out twigs and string. Each person makes them into a cross by wrapping the string around the twigs and making a knot (see instructions on page 72). Younger children (and perhaps others!) may need help.

When all the crosses have been made, get everyone to hold their own cross and close their eyes. Get them to feel the cross in their hands and remember how Jesus died for them. Encourage them to say prayers of thanks to Jesus for this.

Sharing bread
A prayer activity for all ages

You will need: flat bread or pittas, or the recipe to make your own chapattis (below)

If you have an oven on site and it is convenient to do so, everyone could help make chapattis for this activity.

With the bread ready in front of you, ask everyone to listen while you remind them of how Jesus ate a last supper with his friends before he died. Read Luke 22:19,20. Explain that Jesus was sharing the Passover meal with his friends. Remind them that Passover is held to celebrate the fact that God set his people free. Say that on the night before he died, Jesus gave his friends a new meal to celebrate – he said they were to share bread as a way of remembering him.

Give everyone a piece of bread. (Have gluten-free bread also available if anyone needs it.) Encourage the children to spend some time silently remembering that Jesus died so we could be free to know God. If appropriate, they can now eat the bread.

Chapattis

Ingredients
450 g/1 lb wholemeal plain flour
250 ml/9 fl oz cold water

How to make
1. Place 250 g of flour in a deep bowl.
2. Fill another bowl with the cold water.
3. A little at a time, add the water to flour, kneading as you go. Continue until your dough is soft and elastic.
4. Sprinkle some of the rest of the flour onto a table.
5. Split your dough into eight slightly flattened balls.
6. Put one on your floured table and roll it out until it's around 15 cm (6 inches) across.
7. Heat a shallow frying pan (you won't need oil for a non-stick pan) and cook the chapatti for about 20–30 seconds or until the surface is bubbling.
8. Turn it over carefully with tongs and cook the other side for 10–15 seconds. It is done when brown spots appear on the underside.
9. Repeat with the rest of the dough.

Pray in the garden
An opportunity for younger children to pray outdoors as Jesus did in Gethsemane

You will need: access to outdoor space and extra adult supervision if necessary

If you have access to an outdoor space (preferably a garden), go outside with the children. Look around at the beautiful things God has made. If this is not possible, encourage the children to imagine they are in a garden. What sort of things might they see?

Tell the story of Jesus praying in Gethsemane

(Mark 14:32–42). You will find a suitable version on page 33 entitled 'In the garden with Jesus'.

After the story, ask the children what sort of prayers they could pray in a garden. They might suggest thanking God for the beautiful flowers and trees. Thank God now, or pray in whatever way the children suggest.

Say that in the Bible story, Jesus prayed in a garden. He prayed a 'please' prayer. Suggest you do that now. What would the children like to ask God for?

Assure the children that they can talk to God about anything, anywhere.

Creative prayer for what Jesus has done
A responsive prayer for Easter Day

You will need: the words of the prayer projected on PowerPoint/OHP or printed on the service sheet

Explain that the events of Good Friday and Easter Sunday give both a reason to be cheerful, and also a responsibility. This congregational prayer gives us an opportunity to thank Jesus for what he has done for us and for the task he has given us.

Leader: For dying in our place,
All: We thank you, Lord Jesus.
Leader: For enduring the pain of the cross,
All: We thank you, Lord Jesus.
Leader: For appearing to your disciples, alive and well,
All: We thank you, Lord Jesus.
Leader: For taking away doubts and fear,
All: We thank you, Lord Jesus.
Leader: For sending us out to tell the world,
All: We thank you, Lord Jesus.

Party popper praise
An Easter praise activity for all ages together

You will need: two party poppers for each person in the congregation

Distribute the party poppers and explain that they will be used to help celebrate Jesus' resurrection, in prayer. Teach the congregation the response 'Lord Jesus, we celebrate that you rose from the dead and are with us now.'

Split the congregation into sections (choose how many is appropriate, according to the size of your congregation) and explain that you will address each section in turn with the words 'Lord God, on this day we remember the words of your messenger to those women who came to Jesus' tomb in search of his body, "He has risen! He is not here!"' Each section of the congregation should respond by repeating the learned response words and then letting off one of their party poppers (taking care to aim them upwards to avoid causing injury to others). When this pattern has been followed for all the sections of the congregation, use the same words of address to the whole congregation. They should then respond all together with the words of the learned response and by setting off their second party popper (again, taking care not to cause injury to others).

If you have a large congregation you could encourage them to shout or clap instead of using party poppers.

Prayer flags
An Easter praise activity for all ages together

You will need: paper cut into triangles, thin garden canes, sticky tape, pens and crayons

Cut enough long, thin triangle shapes from the paper for everyone to have one. Distribute the shapes and pens and invite everyone to write a short prayer of praise or thanksgiving, on their triangle, for the good news of Easter. Younger children could express their praise by decorating the triangle with colours. Each triangle should then be stuck to a garden cane to create a 'prayer flag' that can be waved during the singing of celebratory Easter songs.

DIY poetry praise
A prayer activity for young people and/or adults in a small-group situation

You will need: a flip chart or large sheet of paper, pens, paper, ambient music, CD or MP3 player with speakers, musical instruments (optional)

Ask the group to suggest key words or phrases

that, in their view, sum up what Jesus achieved by dying on the cross and rising again. Note the words or phrases on the flip chart.

Now encourage everyone to turn the words or phrases into a poem of four-word lines that describe what Jesus has done. The kind of lines you're looking for are:

People lover, Sacrifice maker,
Enemy forgiver, Soul searcher,
Death defeater, Life provider,
Hope giver, Heaven opener.

Turn the poem into praise and thanksgiving. Play the ambient music quietly in the background and begin the praise with 'Jesus, thank you for dying on the cross. We praise you...' – either get other people to repeat the poem phrases or do so yourself.

If you have a musically gifted group, you could perhaps get them to create their own percussion and instrumentals to go along with the words. Think how you might present it to others, to help them worship the risen Jesus, if the opportunity arises.

Prayer steps
A prayer activity based on Luke 24:13–35 for children aged 8+

You will need: percussion instrument (optional)

Ask each child to write down on paper the exciting news about Jesus coming back to life again. Make sure that everyone has made a contribution even if an adult helper has written down their words for them. Collect all the contributions.

Organise the children to stand in a circle and practise taking 11 steps around the circle in time to the beat of the percussion instrument or rhythmic clapping. This represents the 11 kilometres to Emmaus. Now explain that you will read the good news statements out, one at a time, after each walk of 11 steps. Encourage the group to listen carefully in a meditative way.

Each time they walk 11 steps, sound the beat a little faster. Finally, encourage the children to shout: 'Jesus is alive!'

Picture prayer

Creative prayer for Easter

A response to the story of Thomas for children aged 8+

You will need: a copy of page 73 for each child

Invite everyone to listen to a retelling of John 20:19–31 or read these verses from a modern translation. Give each child a copy of page 73. Invite them to look at the expressions in each of the 'photos'. Ask which photo is most like how they are feeling at the moment. Are they excited because Jesus is alive? Are they not sure about Jesus? Do they want to say 'My Lord and my God' to Jesus?

Invite them to fold their sheet along the dotted lines until they can only see the one 'photo' that expresses how they feel. Encourage them to find a space and talk to Jesus on their own, and tell him why they have chosen that particular picture. If appropriate, invite any children who would like you to pray with them to join you.

Responsive prayer
A responsive Easter prayer for younger children or all ages together

Everyone can say 'We praise you, Jesus' after each line.
You are alive.
We praise you, Jesus.
You let your disciples see you.
We praise you, Jesus.
You let your disciples touch you.
We praise you, Jesus.
You let your disciples watch you eat.
We praise you, Jesus.
You proved you had really come back to life.
We praise you, Jesus.
You are alive and with us today.
We praise you, Jesus.

Thank you for Easter!
An action prayer for children aged 2–5

Teach the children the actions to this prayer:

Jesus, *(Point upwards.)*
You love me. *(Point to yourself.)*
I'm so happy *(Use your index finger to draw a big smile on your face.)*
You are here. You are alive today *(Jump up high.)*
And I can shout, *(Put your hands to your mouth.)*
'Thank you for Easter!' *(Shout!)*

Practise the words and actions and then use these as a prayer. Repeat them, changing the words to 'us' and 'we' to give a group feeling to the prayer.

Sad then happy
A responsive prayer for younger children

This prayer acknowledges that the story of Jesus' death makes us sad. Tell the children that, however we feel, we can always talk to God. You are going to do that now. Ask the children to say 'Thank you, God' with you each time. Practise saying these words together before you start.

Dear God, what a sad story we heard today, but you can make sad things happy.
Thank you, God.

When Jesus died, it was very sad, but you can make sad things happy.
Thank you, God.

But, Father God, you made Jesus come alive again!
Thank you, God.

Now Jesus is alive for ever! Hurray!
Thank you, God.

Activity on page 65

Creative prayer

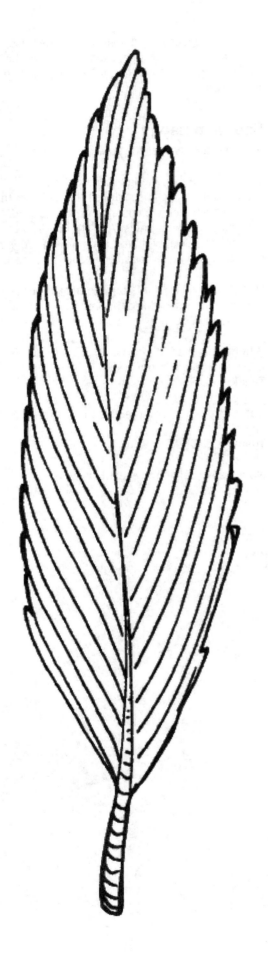
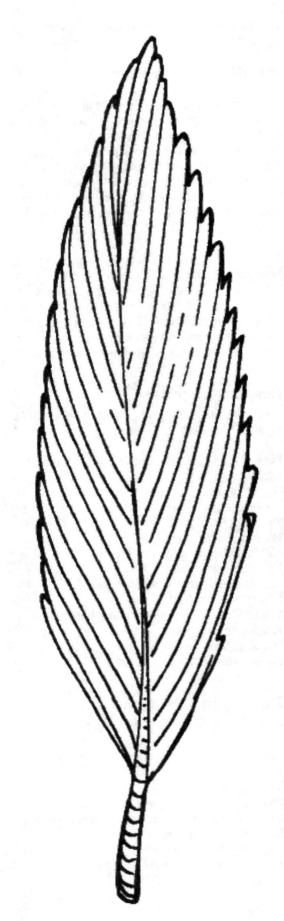

70

Prayer wheel

Activity on page 66

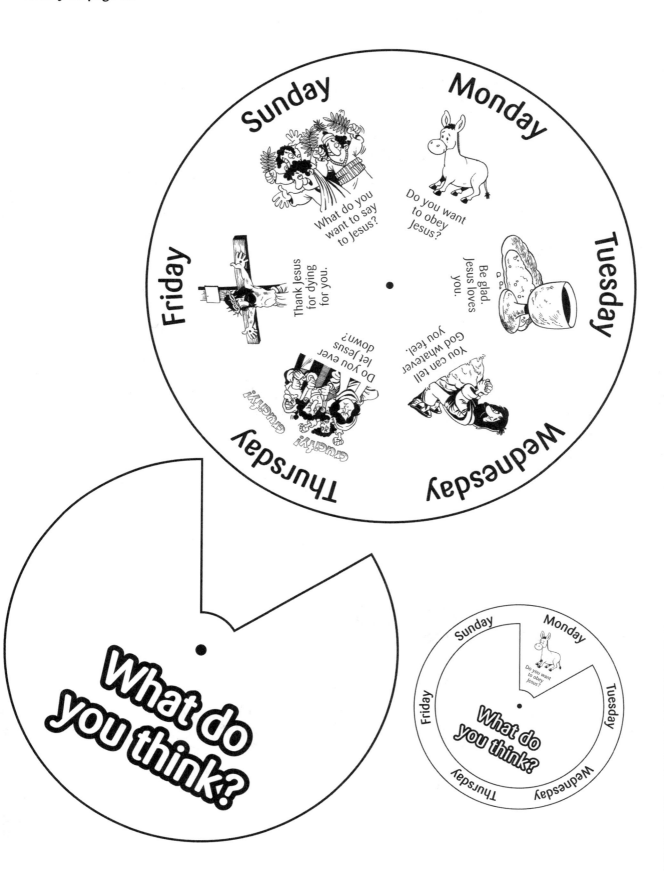

1. Lay two twigs in the shape of a cross on top of some string.

2. Tie the string in a tight knot over the twigs.

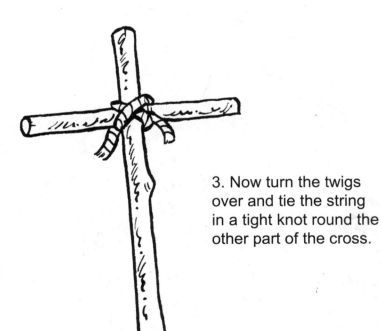

3. Now turn the twigs over and tie the string in a tight knot round the other part of the cross.

Creative prayer

Picture prayers

Activities on pages 69 and 82

Eleven games for different age-groups to bring Easter themes to life

Easter eggs

An activity for young people aged 11+ to help them see the value of what happened at Easter time

You will need: eggs (hard-boiled and painted), chocolate egg prize

Before the session, paint a large number of hard-boiled eggs in different colours, including one sprayed just with gold paint. Work out a scoring system whereby each colour of egg has a value. So, for example, each blue egg is worth 10 points, each green egg is worth 15. You could include bonus points for having a certain number of one colour but, whatever you do, give the gold egg a minus score!

Hide the eggs and then send the group out egg hunting. Explain that as they find the eggs, they can swap them with each other. Don't tell them your scoring system, but say that they have to guess the value of the eggs based on their colours and collect those that they think hold the highest value. Because there is only one gold egg, they are likely to want to barter for that one!

Once all the eggs have been found, gather the young people back together and ask them to count up how many of each colour egg they have.

At this point, explain the scoring system and get the young people to add up their scores. Give a chocolate egg to the person with the most points.

Explain that it's usually better to know whether things are valuable or not before we invest in them. Challenge the young people to look at the Easter story in the light of this. Finish by explaining to the group the importance of Jesus' death and resurrection for Christians: they are the focal point of the whole purpose of God with the human race. His death like a common criminal might have seemed worthless and pointless, but Jesus didn't stay a dead sacrifice for long – because he never sinned, death couldn't hold him. He's alive and his resurrection means that those who believe in him are saved from the punishment their sins deserve, and will be raised to life after death. What should our response be?

A restricted game

A game suitable for Palm Sunday for young people aged 11+

You will need: equipment for your chosen game.

Choose one of these games depending on your group and venue to introduce the idea that Jesus came to bring freedom:

Play an active game such as football, but restrict everyone by playing in pairs (like a three-legged race) or making everyone play with their hands holding on to their ankles.

Play a card or board game such as 'Snap' or 'Snakes and Ladders', but restrict players by tying their wrists to another player's with a length of string.

Introduce the game, divide the young people into small teams as necessary and explain the restrictions to them. Allow them to play the game for a while and then let them play it without the restrictions.

Discuss what it's like to be restricted like this. Then, explain that Jesus was welcomed into Jerusalem as a king because the people thought he would free them from Roman rule. However, Jesus' mission to earth wasn't to save the Jews from the Romans; it was to save everyone from sin and make it possible for us to have a relationship with God. This came as a bit of a shock to the Jews. But Jesus was never restricted by what people expected of him. He was free to do what God wanted.

Pin the tail

A variation on the well-known game, for older children or young people

You will need: the picture of Jesus sitting on a donkey from page 77, cut-out pictures of a cloak, a palm branch and a tail, sticky tack, a blindfold, a small prize

This is a variation on the game 'Pin the tail on the donkey'. Each player is blindfolded and then challenged to place the tail on the donkey, the cloak on the road in front of the donkey and the palm branch in the hands of the crowd. The one who gets nearest to all three wins a prize!

Games

Themed games for Easter

Egg-rolling

An Easter game for older children, to introduce the idea that God had a plan through the life and death of Jesus

You will need: chocolate eggs, obstacle course, a timer

The aim of this timed challenge is for teams to roll their eggs around an obstacle course quickly. Create an interesting course and organise your group to work in teams of three or four.

Give every child an egg and explain that each team has to roll all their eggs from start to finish. Everyone has to be involved. No one is allowed to move their feet while holding an egg or hold more than one egg at a time. Say that success relies on having a good time-saving plan in which everyone works as a team. Give the children a few minutes to discuss their plan.

Time each attempt. Discuss which plan worked best. Eat the eggs. (You may wish to provide an alternative for children who can't eat chocolate.) Say that at times Jesus' friends might have thought that God was no longer in control, but in fact he had an amazing plan which he worked out through the things that happened to Jesus.

Mime game

A game for older children, to review the events of Holy Week and Easter

You will need: a room with four walls

Ask the children to suggest the four most important events of the Easter story.

Encourage everyone to stand in a space and to think of an action that illustrates each of the events suggested, for example:
Palm Sunday: mime riding on a donkey; wave imaginary palm branches
The Last Supper: mime breaking bread and drinking from a cup
Jesus' arrest in the Garden of Gethsemane: mime drawing imaginary sword; 'sleeping' with head on hands (as the disciples)
Jesus' crucifixion and death: hold both arms out and bow head as if on a cross; point to imaginary nail marks on palms of hands
Jesus' resurrection: curl up in a small ball then gradually stretch out and jump up; mime peering inside the 'cave' and looking surprised

Now allocate one wall to each event. Shout out the name of each event in a random order. Everyone should run to the appropriate wall and do the corresponding action.

For each event choose the best action. In pairs, encourage the children to practise telling each other the Easter story using these actions.

Easter egg relay

A game for older children, to encourage them to think about the meaning of Easter

You will need: small foil-wrapped Easter eggs, teaspoons, chairs and tables for obstacle course

Get the children to arrange an obstacle course using chairs and tables. Divide the children into teams and give each team an egg.

Ask the children what clues they think eggs give us about the Easter story. (Many people share eggs as a symbol of new life. The new life of a baby chick represents the new life offered by Jesus. Some eggs are hollow as a reminder of the empty tomb.)

Challenge the teams to carry an egg on a teaspoon over the obstacle course in relay. You might want to time them or count the number of times the egg is dropped, to establish a winner.

Rescue game

An active game for older children

You will need: a large space

One child is the 'guard' and a second child is the 'prisoner'. The 'guard' stands facing the wall with the 'prisoner' beside him. The other children stand at the far end of the room. The children move toward the 'guard', to rescue the 'prisoner'. When the 'guard' turns round they must stand completely still. Anyone who the 'guard' sees moving becomes a prisoner as well.

If someone manages to get to any of the 'prisoners' and touches them, that child and all the other children run back to the start. The 'guard' chases them, and anyone who is caught before they reach the far wall is taken 'prisoner' again.

After the game, ask the children if they would

be prepared to rescue someone if they knew they might be caught in the process? How much danger would they be prepared to put themselves in, in order to rescue someone else? Challenge them to think about the danger Jesus faced in order to rescue us.

Missing piece

A game for younger children to help them see the central meaning of the cross in Jesus' life

You will need: a copy of the pictures on page 78 cut out for each child

Give each child a set of pictures, keeping back the cross pieces. See how fast they can put the pictures in order, showing what Jesus did on earth.

If they don't notice, ask if an important picture is missing, and give them all a cross piece. Invite everyone to take it in turns to say something about Jesus' life using a picture. Remind the children that everything Jesus did was part of God's plan, including his death on the cross.

Message game

An Easter game for under-5s

Play a simple message-passing game, based on Thomas' experiences (John 20:19–29). (A suitable version of this story can be found in *The Big Bible Storybook* page 215 or in this book on page 27 entitled 'My best friend Jesus'.

Say the first phrase of the message below to the child next to you; let him or her pass the message around the group until it gets back to you. Repeat with other phrases. This game will work well for children who can talk confidently.

Jesus is alive.
How do you know?
I've seen him.
Yes, Jesus is really alive!

Put Jesus on the donkey

A simple version of 'Pin the tail' for under-5s suitable for Palm Sunday

You will need: a poster of a large donkey and a separate Jesus shape (see page 79), sticky tack

Adapt the traditional game of 'Pin the tail on the donkey' to 'Put Jesus on the donkey'. Let the children take it in turns to stand near the donkey poster, close their eyes and then stick the Jesus shape (with a piece of sticky tack) on the donkey. When they open their eyes again, they can see if they have managed it. Keep the game fun and non-competitive: for such young children, this will give enough challenge and interest.

As you play the game together, take opportunities to talk about how Jesus entered Jerusalem, who Jesus is, why he was on the donkey, and so on.

Memory game

A 'Last Supper' game for under-5s

You will need: play food, bread, cup, cloth

Help the children remember what Jesus said at his last meal with his disciples with this simple game.

Put a few items of play food on the table or floor, together with some bread and a cup. Name the objects with the children as you point to them. Then cover them with a cloth and, discreetly, remove the bread.

Take off the cloth and ask the children if they can remember what is missing. Prompt the children that it was something that Jesus told them to remember him by. Produce the bread and remind the children that Jesus said, 'When you eat bread, remember me.' Put the bread back under the cloth.

Repeat with the cup. Again remind the children that Jesus said, 'When you drink wine, remember me.' Put the cup back.

Next time remove the bread and the cup. Can the children remember what Jesus said at his last meal?

Pin the tail

Activity on page 74

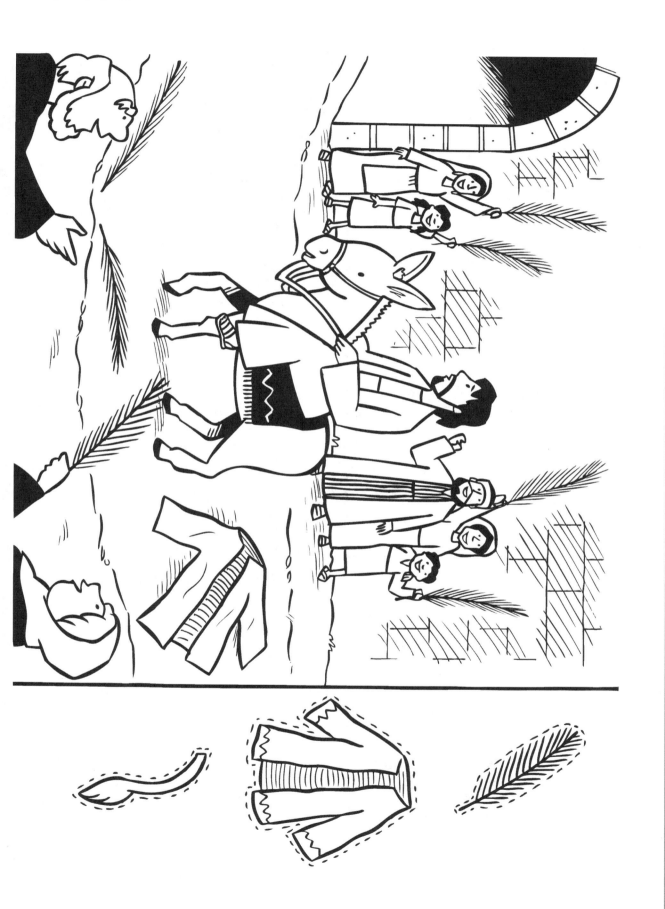

Activity on page 76

Games

78

Put Jesus on the donkey

Activity on page 76

A page of food ideas to enhance your Easter events

As with all food preparation and cooking activities, please ensure good hygiene standards and be aware of food allergies.

Sensory experiences

If your session or service is based on a Gospel account which mentions bread (for example, The Last Supper, the walk to Emmaus or the breakfast on the beach), you could think of a way to get the smell of freshly baked bread into the meeting place (for example, heat some bread in a nearby kitchen, bring in hot bread rolls or bring an electric bread maker). This provides a memorable sensory experience. If drinks are served after or during the session, serve freshly baked bread rolls instead of biscuits.

Bread initials

In a session based on Luke 24:13–35 (the walk to Emmaus) either at the start of your session or service, or afterwards in an informal social time, give the opportunity for anyone who wishes to make their initials out of bread dough. Bake the shapes before everyone leaves if possible, or they could be baked and frozen for collection at the next opportunity. (Provide paper bags rather than plastic ones if the bread is to be taken home warm.) Older children and adults may be able to understand that the personal nature of each piece of baking reminds us all of our individual need to recognise Jesus. Younger children will simply have a memory of the service that utilises the senses of sight, smell, taste and touch.

Easter biscuits

Preheat the oven to 180 °C, 350 °F, gas mark 4

Ingredients:
340 g self-raising flour
1 teaspoon mixed spice
1 teaspoon cinnamon
175 g butter
175 g sugar
110 g currants
2 beaten eggs

Method:
Put the flour, mixed spice and cinnamon in a bowl and rub in the butter until the mixture resembles breadcrumbs.
Stir in the sugar and currants, add the beaten eggs and knead to a dough.
Roll out to a thickness of 0.5 cm on a floured board.

Cut into biscuits with a pastry cutter.
Place on a baking sheet and bake for 15–20 minutes until golden brown.

Easter nests

Make Easter nests by coating cornflakes or bran flakes with melted chocolate and spooning into paper cases. Place two or three mini eggs in the centre of each nest. Leave to cool before eating.

Broken biscuits

A simple activity for children after they have heard the good news of the Easter message

Divide into groups of up to six children to make a sweet treat using broken biscuits. The recipes given do not require any heating.

Cream 50 g soft margarine with 8 tablespoons condensed milk. Place 11 digestive biscuits into a sealed freezer bag and crush them with a wooden spoon. Stir the crushed biscuits into the mixture with 50 g desiccated coconut (or 50 g crushed cornflakes) and 25 g drinking chocolate. Roll into log shapes and coat with vermicelli.

Talk about how Jesus' 'broken body' was good news for us all and how good news makes people happy. Say that sharing these sweets made from broken biscuits can make others happy too.

Hot cross buns

An activity for younger children to review the Easter story

You will need: hot cross buns (or biscuits with tubes of icing or squeezy cheese)

Show the children the hot cross buns and ask if any of them have ever tasted one. Point out the shape on the top of the bun and say that it reminds us that Jesus died on the cross. Talk about the shape of the bun being like the stone that was in front of the grave. Can the children remember what happened to the stone? What had happened to Jesus?

Sing this song to the tune of 'Hot cross buns':
He's alive! He's alive!
Jesus died upon the cross,
Now he's alive!

Repeat, but change the second line to 'Jesus came alive again'. Eat the buns and think about what happened at Easter.

Group activities

These ideas encourage different age-groups to engage with Easter themes

Headline event

A group activity for young people aged 11+ to help them learn why Jesus was crucified and to rediscover the awe of the resurrection

You will need: copies of page 83, pens, paper, Bibles

Tell the young people that they are going to create a newspaper article on the events of the Easter story. Split the group into two halves. Get one half to read John 19:17–30 looking at the crucifixion, while the other half should read John 20:1–18 focusing on the resurrection.

Distribute copies of page 83. Alternatively, use blank sheets of paper. Get the young people to look at the newspaper template. In pairs, challenge them to work out an exciting headline and the main story for the front page, including interviews with some of the disciples and bystanders in the passage they looked at.

Give them time to use their imagination to fill in the other boxes on the page. Then get everyone to share their ideas around so that they can see what each other has done.

Did any of the groups use words that showed the 'amazingness' and awesomeness of the event? Say that we might know these stories too well now to be surprised or shocked at them, but if a tabloid newspaper reported the events new today, what sort of language do the young people think would be used to cover this amazing event?

Song critique

A group activity for young people aged 11+ to provide a new perspective on the meaning of the crucifixion

You will need: hymn or song books or printouts of lyrics

Many songs and hymns have been written about Jesus' crucifixion. Before the session, pick out a few to look at together. You should have enough for one between every two or three young people. Suitable songs could include: 'Come and see'; 'Come, see the beauty of the Lord'; 'Jesus Christ, I think upon your sacrifice'; 'Led like a lamb to the slaughter'; 'There is a green hill far away'.

Divide the young people into pairs or threes, provide hymn/song books or printed lyrics and allocate one of the songs to each group.

Ask them to think about the reasons for Jesus' death and then to consider the song or hymn. Does it do justice to the reasons? Are there other reasons that the hymn mentions? Once they have critiqued the hymn, ask them to try to improve it, write a new verse or even write their own song or poem, giving thanks for Jesus' sacrifice.

Self-evaluation

An activity to encourage young people aged 11+ to think through their own reasons for believing that Jesus is alive

You will need: a copy of page 84 for each person, pens, Bibles

Read Luke 24:1–43 as a group. Ask the group to point out as many instances in the passage as they can where Jesus' followers had an opportunity to believe that he was alive.

Hand out copies of the self-evaluation form. Divide the young people into pairs and encourage them to complete their forms. Allow those who wish to do so to work alone.

Ask the group to share what symbol they think represents them and why. Make the point that it took Jesus to appear in physical form before his followers believed, so those who struggle to believe should not feel bad.

Finish by encouraging some of the young people to share their reasons for believing that Jesus is alive. If you need to, share why you believe.

Good news message

A group activity for children aged 8+ to make a way of sharing the good news of Easter

You will need: old newspapers, scissors, large sheets of paper, glue sticks

Invite the children to share the good news that they have discovered about Jesus with others. Give out some old newspapers and scissors. Help the children to cut out individual words and letters from the headlines and paste them onto a new sheet to make up an Easter message, for example: 'Jesus is alive today. Not dead, but risen. Celebrate new life at Easter.'

Invite everyone to take their sheets home and pin them up in a place where they will be noticed.

Bible photos

An activity for children aged 8+ to encourage them to have faith in Jesus

You will need: a copy for each child of page 73, copies of the SU booklet *Me + Jesus* (ISBN 978 1 84427 142 9)

In advance, cut up the pictures on page 73, making one set for each child.

Ask the children to line up in order of hair colour, with the child with the darkest hair at one end and the child with the lightest hair at the other. When they are in line, ask them how they achieved this. Next, ask the children to line up in age order with the youngest at one end and the oldest at the other. When they are in line, ask them how they achieved this. For the first line they will have looked at each other to compare, and for the second they will have asked each other their dates of birth. However, they had no real evidence for when someone's birthday was – they had to believe that they were being told the truth. Explain that in the Bible story they are about to hear there is a person who didn't believe what his friends had told him.

Give each child a set of pictures. Say that these are pretend photos of an event in the Bible. In pairs, invite the children to look at each picture and briefly discuss what they think it shows. Challenge them to put the images in the right order as they hear the story. (They are in the correct order on the page.)

Read John 20:24–30 to the children, from the Bible. As you read, try to imagine you were there. It will help to convey the excitement of the disciples as they tell Thomas what they have seen and his response when he finally sees the risen Jesus for himself.

Allow a few moments of silence for the children to absorb what they have heard. Invite any children who would like to, to tell everyone what they think God wants us to know from this story. It's all about Jesus, but what about him? And why do we need to know this?

Run through the correct order for the 'photos' and encourage the children to stick them on a sheet of plain paper. Challenge them to draw another 'photo' showing their reaction to this story – do they believe what they heard or not? Invite them to write a short prayer to God asking him to help them have faith in Jesus. They could stick this 'photo album' on their wall at home to encourage them to keep praying the words of their prayer.

If appropriate, share with the children when you said to Jesus, 'You are my Lord and my God'. Ask if it is something they have ever done, or would like to do. Invite them to chat with you after the session if they want to know more. Have copies of the SU booklet *Me + Jesus* to look at with any children who are interested.

Bulbs, seeds and flowers

An activity for younger children to help them understand God's plan in sending Jesus to die for us

You will need: some bulbs or seeds and corresponding flowers or pictures of flowers, for example, daffodils (Be aware that some bulbs can irritate the skin.)

Ask: 'What has to happen for a bulb to grow into a flower?' (*Be buried*). Say that this is a bit like what happened to Jesus – his dead body was buried. As each person holds a bulb, suggest they silently thank Jesus for dying as part of his plan to rescue us.

Ask the children what happens to the buried bulbs (*they grow into flowers*). Say this reminds us of the amazing part of Jesus' rescue plan, where he came alive after being buried. Before they leave, let each child exchange their bulb for a flower to remind themselves at home that Jesus is alive.

Headline event

Activity on page 81

Jerusalem ✡ Star

Headline:

Lead article:

Interviews:

Tabloid filler:

Picture:

Activity on page 81

Proof

If you look back at Luke 24 you will note that the were five main instances of proof for Jesus' followers to believe that was alive: the empty tomb (vs 2,3), the angels (vs 4–7), the Scriptures (v 27), Jesus' actions (v 30) and Jesus in physic form (v 40). Read the verses then decide which of these descriptions fits you best.
Then think of some reasons for your choice.

An empty tomb

You are someone who doesn't need much convincing that Jesus is alive and answers prayer. You believe that Jesus is alive because you see God moving and answering prayers in most things.

Angels

You are someone who is open to God's signs and wonders, but it often takes something big to really convince you. You see most things of a supernatural nature as proof of God.

The Scriptures

You are someone who believes that Jesus is alive because it is written in the Bible. You very rarely question the reliability of the Bible even if you don't understand it.

Jesus' actions

You are someone who needs more obvious and direct miracles to believe. You can't help but be suspicious of most miracles and you have big questions about the reliability of th Bible.

Jesus in physical form

It would take Jesus himself to appear in physical form and show you his hands for yo to believe.

Missing words puzzle

Find the missing words in the grid or in Matthew 21:1–17. After you have copied the word in a square into the space, shade in that square.

The prophets (verses 4,5)

Zechariah
God told me to say these words. Your _ _ _ _ (A1) will come to you, riding on a _ _ _ _ _ _ (E5).
God told me to say this, so you can expect it to happen!

Isaiah
God told me that his house, or _ _ _ _ _ _ (B1), would be a place of _ _ _ _ _ _ _ (E1) for all nations. God told me to say this, so you can expect it to happen!

Two disciples (verses 1–3,6)
Jesus told us to come to this village and look for _ _ _ (D3) donkeys. He said that the owner would just let us take them. We had to say "The _ _ _ _ (A4) needs them". Jesus told us to do this, so we expected it to happen.

The crowd
Everyone was throwing their coats on the _ _ _ _ (D1). We were _ _ _ _ _ _ _ _ (D5) praises to God. "He's a king like David! God bless him!" We expect that he'll become our king.

Chief priests
It was the Passover festival so we expected lots of visitors in _ _ _ _ _ _ _ _ _ (B4). We expected them to buy doves and change _ _ _ _ _ (A3) at the temple. It's our law. We expect that Jesus will cause trouble.

The temple traders
We expected a busy day of _ _ _ _ _ _ (B5) and _ _ _ _ _ _ _ (E3). We never expected what happened next. He turned over our _ _ _ _ _ _ (B3) and drove us out!

Jesus
I expected to find a place where people could _ _ _ _ (E4) and meet God. I found noise and buying and selling. I had to take action, to make the temple into God's _ _ _ _ _ (D4). Then people could come and be _ _ _ _ _ _ (A5).

	A	B	C	D	E
1	king	temple	help	road	worship
2	amazing	best	thanks	brilliant	the one
3	money	tables	sorry	two	selling
4	Lord	Jerusalem	please	house	pray
5	healed	buying	praise	shouting	donkey

What would happen next?
The people expected Jesus to be their king.
The chief priests expected trouble.
And Jesus? He already knew where he would be in just a few days' time.
(The squares that you haven't used will give you a clue.)
Jesus turned over the tables so that people could have a place to meet with God. He turned over all the wrong things that keep us away from God, so that we can meet with God in our everyday lives.
What do you want to say to God about this?
The words inside the cross may help you, or use your own words.

Read the story then find the bold words in the wordsearch!

Jesus and his friends were in an **upstairs** room celebrating the **Passover** together.
"I've really looked forward to sharing this **supper** with you before I enter my time of suffering." said Jesus.
He took some **bread,** gave **thanks** and broke it. Then he shared the bread with the whole group.
"This bread is like my **body, given** for you. Eat it in my **memory**."
The disciples looked at each other, confused. They weren't quite sure what Jesus meant.

Then Jesus took the **cup**. "This cup of **wine** will remind you of the **blood** that's going to be **poured** out for you. One of you who is sitting at this table now is betraying me. God has already decided that I must die, but it is a terrible thing to be the person who **betrays** me."

You can read this story in Luke 22:14–23. Today people celebrate Holy Communion to remember this special last meal that Jesus had with his disciples and to remember how Jesus died for each one of us.

```
D O O L B A M B B G
P A S S O V E R C I
D W U F D G M E A V
I I S K Y L O A R E
M N E B O P R D E N
C E J E R S Y T P U
U P S T A I R S P V
P O U R E D W X U Y
X T H A N K S Z S A
  W B Y C D E F G
    S G I W
    C P
```

Songs, rhymes and poems

For young people and adults

Can I believe?

A poem which could be read to young people or adults, with soft music in the background, to help them reflect on their own response to the risen Christ.

Can I believe, Lord, that you are alive?
Do I know in my heart the joy of the risen Christ?
I will search my heart,
I will search my heart.

Do I feel your presence in my life?
Can I know you love me, died for me and rose again?
I will search my heart,
I will search my heart.

Come to me, Lord, as I give my life to you,
Let me know and feel the joy of your presence in my life.
Then I will praise you, Lord,
Then I will praise you, Lord.
Amen.

Copyright © Jane Wade 2006

That walk

This poem could be read slowly to young people or adults following an exploration of the resurrection story.

Lord, you took that walk to the cross for me,
And as I stand with the disciples in your Resurrection glory,
May I truly know that you live.
That you live in the hearts of men and women today,
That you know me and have called me by name,
That like those first disciples I too am called,
That I am called to follow where you lead,
That I am called to tell all nations about the wonder of your love,
Your forgiving power, your sacrifice,
Made for me,
When you took that walk to the cross.
Copyright © Jane Wade 2007

For children

Look at the cross

A simple explanation in verse of the meaning of the cross for children aged 5+.

Look at the cross.
What do you see?
Something that says
Jesus loves me.

Look at the cross.
What does it say?
That Jesus took
My sins away.

Look at the cross
What does it show?
That Jesus lives
And loves me so.

From *Praise and Pray*
Words: Majory Francis
Music: Kathryn Wright

Jesus died...

A rhyme with actions and movements which tells the Easter story, for under-5s.

Jesus died on a cross. (*Stretch your arms out sideways.*)

His body was put in a grave. (*Lie down on the floor.*)

A big stone was rolled in front of the opening. (*Hold your arms out at the side to make a big, round shape. Then turn round slowly.*)

Jesus' friends came to see his body. (*Walk up and down or on the spot.*)

They were very sad. (*Rub your eyes.*)

But they found the stone was rolled away. (*Make wide arms and turn round again.*)

Where was Jesus? (*Shrug, with your palms upturned.*)

Jesus was alive again! (*Jump up and down and wave your arms.*)

Do this, do this

A song for younger children or all ages together

Iain Whyte
arr. Ruth Wills

Do this, do this and re-mem-ber me, When you share this meal to-ge - ther, Do this, do this and re-mem-ber me, I will be with you for-ev - er. (Do) I. Je - sus eat-ing with his friends in a room in Ga-li - lee, Takes the bread and takes the wine, says 'These things are like me, The bread is for my bo-dy, and the wine is for my blood, I give them both to you my friends a gift from God a - bove.'_____ (Do)

Chorus

2. 'Take the bread and take the wine and share them with me now,
   Pass this celebration on to tell the people how
   I am with you always, so, no matter where you are,
   Just think of me when I am gone and I will hear your pray'r.'

Chorus

3. Now two thousand years have passed and yet we still recall,
   The words of Jesus to his friends that now speak to us all,
   So, we can share this meal today and in the bread and wine,
   We can see the love of God is with us for all time.

Chorus

Let's celebrate

A lively action song for Easter for younger children

Words and music by
Sue Dunn

1. Has your favour - ite team just scored a goal?_ Then ce - le - brate,_ let's
   nat - ional hero just won the race?_ Then ce - le - brate,_ let's

1. ce - le - brate!_ Has the **2.** ce - le - brate! But the great - est thing_ to hap - pen ev - er

since the world_ be - gan is when Je - sus rose from the dead._

Chorus

Ce - le - brate, ce - le - brate, jump up and down,_
He's a - live, he's a - live, jump up and down,_

ce - le - brate, ce - le - brate, turn a - round,_ lift up your hands and
he's a - live, he's a - live, turn a - round,_ lift up your hands and

give him praise, 'cause Je - sus rose from the dead!
give him praise, 'cause Je - sus rose from the dead! *(on D.C.)* 2. Are you

---

Verse 1
Has your favourite team just scored a goal?
(kick an imaginary ball)
Then celebrate, let's celebrate!
Has the national hero just won the race?
(run on the spot)
Then celebrate, let's celebrate!
But the greatest thing to happen ever since the world began
Is when Jesus rose from the dead.

Verse 2
Are you going to a wedding in the family?
(throw confetti)
Then celebrate, let's celebrate!
Have you got a baby brother or a sister now?
(rock a baby)
Then celebrate, let's celebrate!
But the greatest thing to happen ever since the world began
Is when Jesus rose from the dead.

Chorus

Chorus
Celebrate, celebrate, jump up and down,
Celebrate, celebrate, turn around,
Lift up your hands and give him praise,
'Cause Jesus rose from the dead!
He's alive, he's alive, jump up and down,
He's alive, he's alive, turn around,
Lift up your hands and give him praise,
'Cause Jesus rose from the dead!

Verse 3
Are you going somewhere special for a birthday treat?
(arms in the air)
Then celebrate, let's celebrate!
Are you having all your favourite things to eat?
(pretend to eat)
Then celebrate, let's celebrate!
But the greatest thing to happen ever since the world began
Is when Jesus rose from the dead.

Chorus

Clippety-clop!

A story-rhyme based on the Palm Sunday story for under-5s.

Clippety-clop, clippety-clop!
What is that?
It's a little donkey – fancy that!
Trit-trot, trit-trot!
I think he's coming this way!
On his back rides Jesus!
Hurray, hurray, hurray!

Coats off, on the ground, lay them side by side,
Make a special carpet – now see Jesus ride.
Quick, pluck some branches, wave them all about!
Let's all praise King Jesus!
Let's clap and sing and shout!

What would you do?

A 'discussion starter' based on the Palm Sunday story for younger children.

What would you do, what would you say,
If Jesus came along this way?
Would you carry on your play?

What would you do, what would you say,
If Jesus came along this way?
Would you hide or run away?

What would you do, what would you say,
If Jesus came along this way?
Would you stand quite still and pray?

What would you do, what would you say,
If Jesus came along this way?
Would you wave a branch and sway?

What would you do, what would you say,
If Jesus came along this way?
Would you cheer and shout,
'Hooray!'?

Stomp, stomp!

An action rhyme for under-5s.

You will need: a drum (or other percussion instrument)

Ask the children to stand behind a leader who is holding the drum and to march when they hear the drum beat. If you do not have access to a drum or another percussion instrument, clap your hands instead. Encourage the children to repeat the final line of each verse in an expressive way! Say the following rhyme, beating the drum and marching on 'Stomp':

Stomp, stomp, stomp, stomp!
Jesus' friends walked on the dusty road.
Huff! Dusty feet!

Stomp, stomp, stomp, stomp!
Jesus' friends walked in the hot, hot sun.
Ugh! Smelly feet!

Stomp, stomp, stomp, stomp!
Jesus' friends walked on the muddy path.
Ooh! Muddy feet!

Stomp, stomp, stomp, stomp!
Jesus' friends walked down the dirty street.
Yuk! Dirty feet!

Stomp, stomp, stomp, stomp!
Jesus' friends walked a long, long way.
Yawn! Tired feet!

But wait a minute. Who will wash these dusty, smelly, muddy, dirty, tired feet?
Will you?

Repeat the 'Stomp' verses of the marching rhyme again. Then continue:

But wait a minute. Who will wash these dusty, smelly, muddy, dirty, tired feet?
I can see someone who will.
It's Jesus.
He takes a bowl of water and a towel.
He washes the dusty, smelly, muddy, dirty, tired feet of all his friends.
He does it to show that he loves them.

This is the bread

A rhyme about the Last Supper for younger children. Add actions for them to copy.

This is the bread, and this is the wine,
At the last meal.

This is Jesus, who ate the bread
And drank the wine, at his last meal.

These are the friends, who sat with Jesus,
To eat the bread and drink the wine,
At his last meal.

Songs, rhymes and poems

This is the room, where Jesus sat,
With all his friends, to eat the bread
And drink the wine, at his last meal.

This is the man, who showed the way,
To the room upstairs, where Jesus sat,
With all his friends, to eat the bread
And drink the wine, at his last meal.

Gethsemane garden

*Do the actions in italics as you say this rhyme
with younger children.*

Dark night *(peer as if it's very dark)*
Tall trees *(make tree shape with hands)*
Quiet garden *(finger to lips)*
Gentle breeze *(wiggle fingers gently)*

Jesus' friends hear him say, *(hand to ear)*
'Stay awake *(point to eyes)*
While I pray,' *(put hands together)*
But they're tired *(rub eyes)*
They can't do *(shake head)*
What Jesus asks them to.

Mouths yawn *(yawn)*
Heads nod *(nod heads, close eyes)*
While sad Jesus *(make sad face)*
Talks to God *(hands together)*

Suddenly – *(act startled)*
Shouted words! *(flinch as if hearing something
loud)*
NOISY garden, clanking swords *(wave imaginary
sword)*
Judas' kiss *(kiss hand)*

Tells the men 'This one's Jesus – *(point finger)*
Grab him, then!' *(act as if seizing someone)*
Jesus' friends run off home *(make fingers run)*
Leaving Jesus sad, alone. *(shake head and make
a sad face)*

Christine Orme
Let's Sing and Shout
Copyright © Scripture Union 1998

Jesus is alive!

*This rhyme, for younger children, invites them to
celebrate the fact that Jesus is alive.*

Ask the children to stand in a ring. Encourage
them to do the actions as suggested in this
praise rhyme. Pause after each line to allow them
to do the actions.

All join in the repeated line, 'Jesus is alive!' by
jumping up and down.

Stand together in a ring,
Dance around with joy and sing –
Jesus is alive!

Tap your knees and wiggle your hips,
Put a smile upon your lips –
Jesus is alive!

Clap your hands and turn about,
Stamp your feet and then shout out –
Jesus is alive!

Put your arms up high and sway,
Jump up high and shout, 'Hooray!'
Jesus is alive!

He's alive, not dead

*A rhyme for younger children based on John
20:19–29.*

When the friends saw Jesus,
They knew he'd risen from the dead.
'Now we know, we really know
You are alive,' they said.

But Thomas hadn't seen him.
Jesus, he thought, is dead.
'Until I see with my own eyes
I won't believe,' he said.

Then Thomas did see Jesus,
Knew he'd risen from the dead.
He didn't need to touch him.
'My Lord and God,' he said.

Today we can know Jesus,
That he's alive, not dead.
And though we cannot see him,
We're truly blessed, he said.

The story pictures on pages 93 to 96 are for younger children and could be used as handouts for them to colour in. However, ideas are included on this page to make more of the sheets and encourage the children to understand what the pictures mean.

Here comes Jesus

You will need: a copy of the picture on page 93 for each child, crayons

Use this activity after the children have heard the Palm Sunday story (see 'Jesus rides a donkey' on page 32 for a suitable version), to reinforce what they have been discovering. Provide each child with a copy of the picture 'Here comes Jesus' and ask them to tell you who is in it. Give them plenty of time to colour their picture of Jesus on the donkey.

When all the pictures are complete, look at them together and chat about the events of the story. Point out that the pictures all show Jesus on a donkey. Can anyone remember where he was going to on the donkey? What happened when Jesus rode into Jerusalem? What did the people shout out? What did they wave? Encourage all the children to contribute answers.

Look at the pictures again and ask the children to cheer and wave, as the people in the crowd did. Explain that we can feel just as excited today because Jesus is our friend. Cheer and wave again!

A meal with Jesus

You will need: a copy of the picture on page 94 for each child, crayons

You can use the picture 'A meal with Jesus' as an introduction to the story of the Last Supper (see 'A special meal' on page 32 for a suitable version) or to help you review the story together.

Look at the picture and work out what is going on. Identify which person is Jesus. Who are the other people? What are they all doing? What is Jesus holding? Why? Explain that this was an important meal. Jesus and his friends were sharing it together. It is a meal held once a year called the 'Passover' meal.

Ask the children to find the bread and colour it in (or stick on pieces of brown paper). Jesus shared the bread with his friends. He asked them to think about him when they ate bread.

Jesus is holding a cup. Let the children colour or decorate it. Jesus shared the drink with his friends. He asked them to think about him when they drank.

Suggest that the children could think about Jesus next time they eat or drink, just like Jesus' friends did.

A cockerel crows

You will need: a copy of the picture on page 95 for each child, or enlarged copies for group use, crayons, art and craft materials

You can use the picture 'A cockerel crows' as an introduction to the story of Peter's denial (see 'Peter lets Jesus down' in *The Big Bible Storybook* for a suitable version) or to help you review the story together.

This picture lends itself to collage, using real feathers or shaped tissue or crêpe paper to cover the cockerel with bright plumage. If you enlarge the picture, you could make a life-size (or larger than life-size!) bird.

Have the children heard a real cockerel or hen sound? They often make loud crowing noises early in the morning, even before it is daylight! Try making some noisy cockerel sounds together! Suggest the children listen out for a cockerel as you tell the Bible story.

Where is Jesus?

You will need: a copy of the picture on page 96 for each child, or enlarged copies for group use, crayons, art and craft materials

You can use the picture 'Where is Jesus?' as an introduction to the Bible story (see 'What Mary saw' on page 33 for a suitable version) or to help you review the story together.

Show the children the picture and point out the angel in the foreground. Can they say what the angel is pointing at? Remind them that when Jesus died his friends put his body in this place. Ask 'Where is Jesus now?'

Help them to realise that Jesus is no longer in the tomb. He is alive! Encourage them to colour or decorate the picture with collage materials.

A cockerel crows